Business Result

Elementary | Student's Book

David Grant, John Hughes
& Rebecca Turner

Interactive Workbook material
by Alastair Lane and Chris Speck

OXFORD
UNIVERSITY PRESS

Contents

VIDEO : This section of the unit has a video clip linked to the topic.

Introduction

Welcome to *Business Result Elementary*. In this book you will find:
| 12 units | Practice files | Information files | Audio scripts |
| Interactive Workbook on DVD-ROM |

What's in a unit?

Starting point

- an introduction to the unit
- discussion and questions

Working with words

- reading and listening about the world of work
- new words and phrases that you can use in your work
- practise the new words in speaking activities

Language at work

- grammar lessons in real work situations
- helps you communicate better
- practise grammar in the classroom in speaking activities
- for more practice go to the *Practice file*

Practically speaking

- essential words and phrases for general use
- you sound more natural when you speak English

Business communication

- key expressions for exchanging information, socializing, telephoning, travel, and meetings
- real work situations
- *Key expressions* list in every unit

Case study / Activity

- authentic case study, or a communication activity
- role-plays and discussions
- improve your fluency

What's in the Practice file?

Written exercises on the key language in:

- Working with words
- Language at work
- Business communication

plus a language reference section with more grammar explanations.

Use the *Practice file*:

- in class to check your understanding
- after class for extra practice.

Follow the links to the *Practice file* in each unit.

» For more exercises go to **Practice file 3** on page 82.

What's the *Interactive Workbook* on DVD-ROM?

The *Interactive Workbook* lets you practise the language from the *Student's Book*. It also helps you test your own progress. Use it at home or in the office to practise the language you learn in class.

Exercises and Tests

- practise key language with interactive exercises
- check your progress with unit tests

Glossary

- check the meaning of over 300 words and phrases
- listen to the words and add your translation

Phrasebank

- listen to the key expressions from the *Student's Book*
- learn new phrases for exchanging information, socializing, telephoning, travel, and meetings
- create your personal phrasebook

Email

- learn useful phrases for writing emails
- copy example emails to use at work

Listen again

- Listen again to the *Student's Book* audio, or download to your MP3 player

Video

- Watch a video clip related to a section in the unit. Every unit has a video clip which recycles and extends the language of the unit.
- Complete the interactive exercises while you watch the video clips
- This icon **VIDEO** shows you the section of the unit that the video relates to. Watch the video after you have completed the work in the *Student's Book*.

When you see this link, you can go to the *Interactive Workbook* for more practice.

ⓘ » Interactive Workbook »

Fast-track option

If you are on a short course, you can do the fast-track option. For each unit, do *Language at work*, *Practically speaking*, and *Business communication* in class. You can do the other sections in your own time if you wish.

How to use Business Result Elementary | A complete blended learning package

Student's Book | Main unit

In class: Learn vocabulary, grammar, and expressions with listening, reading, and speaking activities.

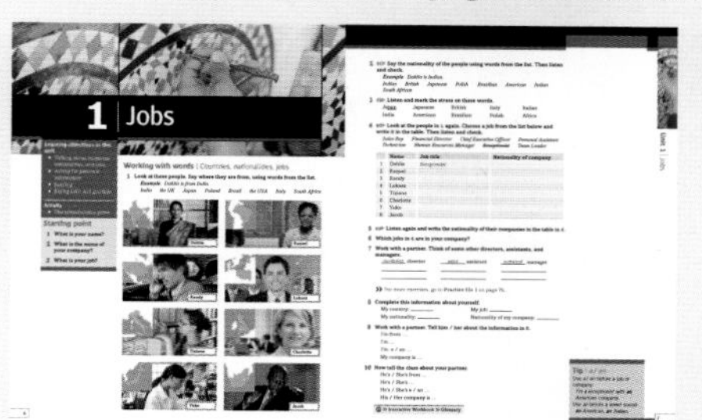
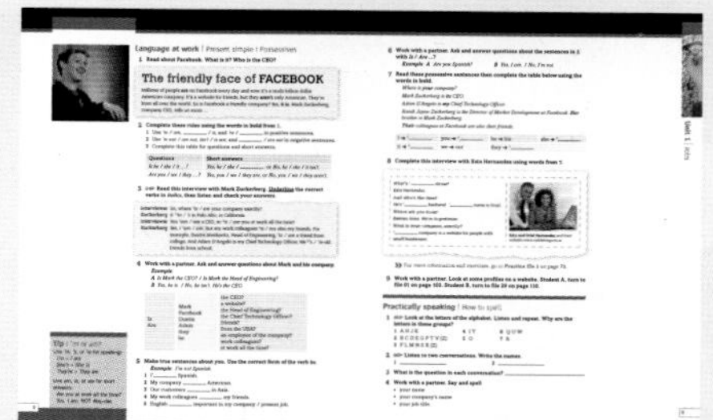
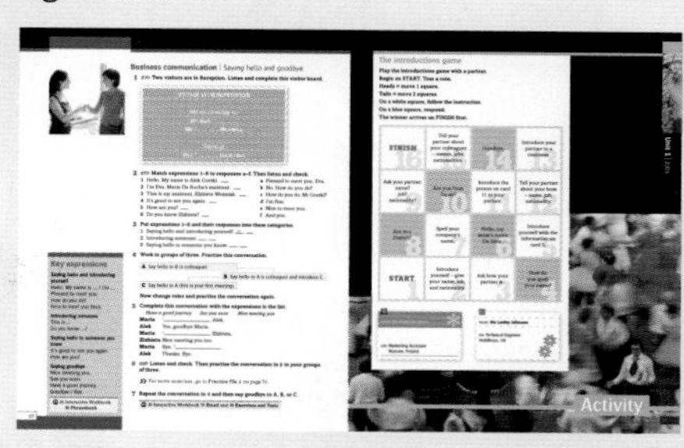

In class **or** self-study: When you see this, go to the *Practice files* at the **back of the book**.

» For more exercises, go to the **Practice files**.

Self-study: When you see this, go to the *Interactive Workbook* on your **DVD-ROM**.

Student's Book | Practice file

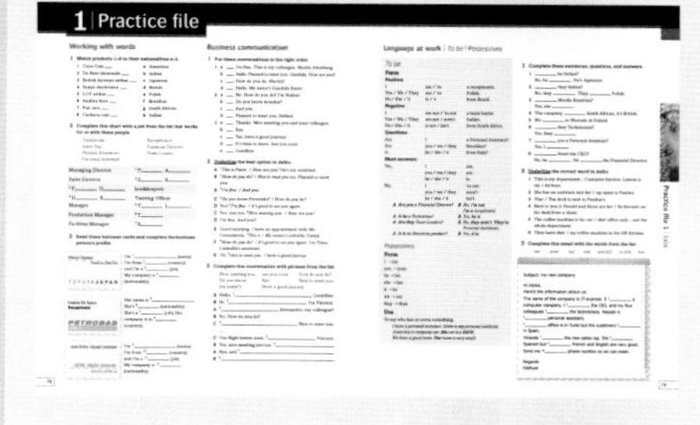

Interactive Workbook

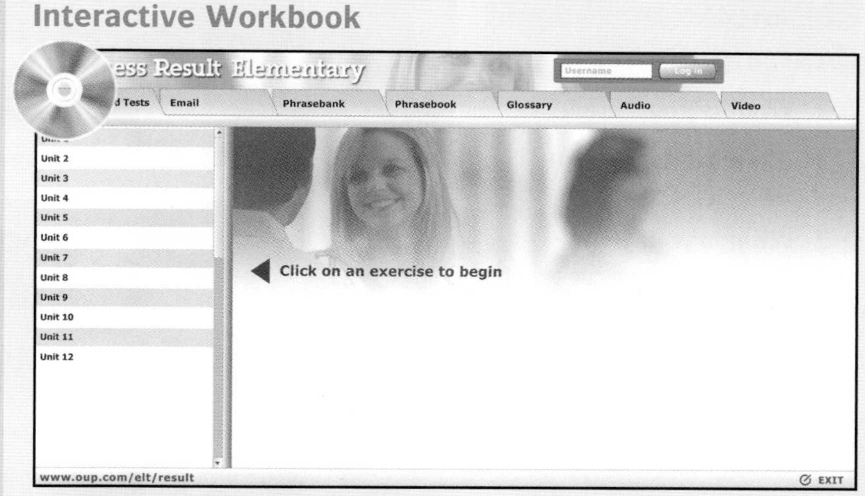

- Exercises & Tests
- Emails
- Phrasebank
- Personal phrasebook
- Glossary
- Student's Book audio
- Video

Business Result online

Self-study: You can access the *Business Result website* by either following the prompts on your **CD-ROM**, or by going to **www.oup.com/elt/result**

Interactive exercises:

- Working with words
- Business communication

Reference material:

- Tips on writing
- Glossaries
- Student's Book grammar explanations
- Practice file answer key

and more ...

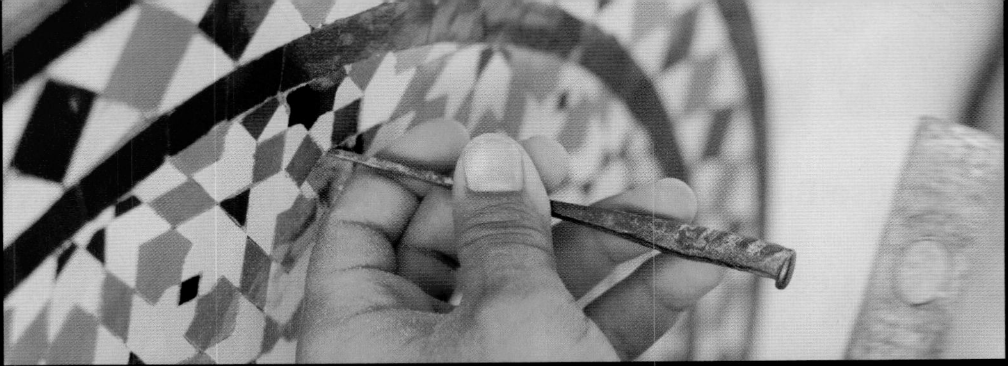

1 Jobs

Learning objectives in this unit

- Talking about countries, nationalities, and jobs
- Asking for personal information
- Spelling
- Saying hello and goodbye

Activity

- The introductions game

Starting point

1 What is your name?

2 What is the name of your company?

3 What is your job?

Working with words | Countries, nationalities, jobs

1 Look at these people. Say where they are from, using words from the list.

***Example**: Dahlia is from India.*

India the UK Japan Poland Brazil the USA Italy South Africa

Dahlia

Raquel

Randy

Lukasz

Tiziana

Charlotte

Yuko

Jacob

2 01▷ **Say the nationality of the people using words from the list. Then listen and check.**

Example: *Dahlia is Indian.*

Indian *British* *Japanese* *Polish* *Brazilian* *American* *Italian* *South African*

3 02▷ **Listen and mark the stress on these words.**

Japan	Japanese	British	Italy	Italian
India	American	Brazilian	Polish	Africa

4 03▷ **Look at the people in 1 again. Choose a job from the list below and write it in the table. Then listen and check.**

Sales Rep *Financial Director* *Chief Executive Officer* *Personal Assistant* *Technician* *Human Resources Manager* *Receptionist* *Team Leader*

	Name	Job title	Nationality of company
1	Dahlia	*Receptionist*	~~Indian~~ American
2	Raquel	Human Resources Manager	Italian
3	Randy	Sales Rep	Japanese
4	Lukasz	Team Leader	Indian
5	Tiziana	Personal Assistant	Polish
6	Charlotte	CHIEF EXECUTIVE	BRITISH
7	Yuko	TECHNICIAN	BRAZILIAN
8	Jacob	FINANCIAL DIRECTOR	SOUTH AFRICAN

5 03▷ **Listen again and write the nationality of their companies in the table in 4.**

6 **Which jobs in 4 are in your company?**

7 **Work with a partner. Think of some other directors, assistants, and managers.**

marketing director   *sales* assistant   *technical* manager

________   ________   ________

________   ________   ________

» For more exercises, go to **Practice file 1** on page 78.

8 **Complete this information about yourself.**

My country: SPAIN   My job: ________

My nationality: SPANISH   Nationality of my company: UNITED KINGDOM

9 **Work with a partner. Tell him / her about the information in 8.**

I'm from …

I'm …

I'm a / an …

My company is …

10 **Now tell the class about your partner.**

He's / She's from …

He's / She's …

He's / She's a / an …

His / Her company is …

ⓘ » Interactive Workbook » **Glossary**

Tip | *a / an*

Use *a / an* before a job or company:

*I'm **a** receptionist with **an** American company.*

Use *an* before a vowel sound:

***an** American, **an** Italian.*

Language at work | Present simple | Possessives

1 Read about Facebook. What is it? Who is the CEO?

The friendly face of FACEBOOK

Millions of people **are** on Facebook every day and now it's a multi-billion dollar American company. It'**s** a website for friends, but they **aren't** only American. They're from all over the world. So is Facebook a friendly company? Yes, **it is**. Mark Zuckerberg, company CEO, tells us more …

2 Complete these rules using the words in bold from 1.

1 Use *'m / am*, ________ / *is*, and *'re* / ________ in positive sentences.
2 Use *'m not / am not, isn't / is not*, and ________ / *are not* in negative sentences.
3 Complete this table for questions and short answers.

Questions	Short answers
Is he / she / it …?	*Yes, he / she /* ________. or *No, he / she / it isn't.*
Are you / we / they …?	*Yes, you / we / they are.* or *No, you / we / they aren't.*

3 04▷ Read this interview with Mark Zuckerberg. <u>Underline</u> the correct verbs in *italics*, then listen and check your answers.

Interviewer So, where [1]*is / are* your company exactly?
Zuckerberg It [2]*'m / 's* in Palo Alto, in California.
Interviewer You [3]*am / are* a CEO, so [4]*is / are* you at work all the time?
Zuckerberg Yes, I [5]*am / are*. But my work colleagues [6]*is / are* also my friends. For example, Dustin Moskovitz, Head of Engineering, [7]*is / are* a friend from college. And Adam D'Angelo is my Chief Technology Officer. We [8]*'s / 're* old friends from school.

4 Work with a partner. Ask and answer questions about Mark and his company.

Example:
A *Is Mark the CEO? / Is Mark the Head of Engineering?*
B *Yes, he is. / No, he isn't. He's the CEO.*

Is Are	Mark Facebook Dustin Adam they he	the CEO? a website? the Head of Engineering? the Chief Technology Officer? friends? from the USA? an employee of the company? work colleagues? at work all the time?

5 Make true sentences about you. Use the correct form of the verb *be*.

Example: *I'm not Spanish.*

1 I'________ Spanish.
2 My company ________ American.
3 Our customers ________ in Asia.
4 My work colleagues ________ my friends.
5 English ________ important in my company / present job.

Tip | *'m* or *am*?

Use *'m*, *'s*, or *'re* for speaking:
I'm = I am
She's = She is
They're = They are

Use *am*, *is*, or *are* for short answers:
Are you at work all the time?
Yes, I am. NOT ~~*Yes, I'm.*~~

6 **Work with a partner. Ask and answer questions about the sentences in 5 with *Is / Are ...*?**

Example: *A* *Are you Spanish?* *B* *Yes, I am. / No, I'm not.*

7 **Read these possessive sentences then complete the table below using the words in bold.**

Where is ***your*** *company?*

Mark Zuckerberg is ***its*** *CEO.*

Adam D'Angelo is ***my*** *Chief Technology Officer.*

Randi Jayne Zuckerberg is the Director of Market Development at Facebook. ***Her*** *brother is Mark Zuckerberg.*

Their *colleagues at Facebook are also their friends.*

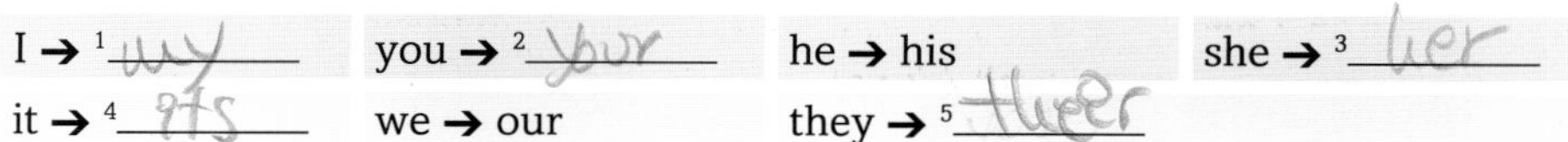

I → [1] ______	you → [2] ______	he → his	she → [3] ______
it → [4] ______	we → our	they → [5] ______	

8 **Complete this interview with Esta Hernandez using words from 7.**

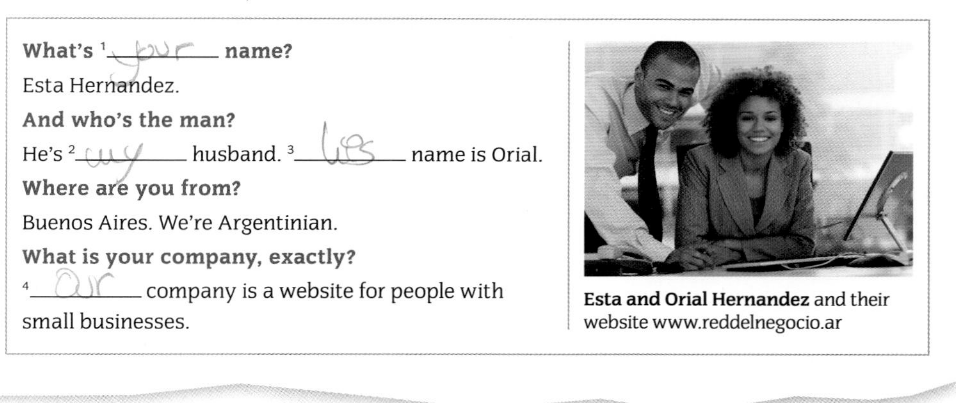

What's [1] ______ name?

Esta Hernandez.

And who's the man?

He's [2] ______ husband. [3] ______ name is Orial.

Where are you from?

Buenos Aires. We're Argentinian.

What is your company, exactly?

[4] ______ company is a website for people with small businesses.

Esta and Orial Hernandez and their website www.reddelnegocio.ar

» For more information and exercises, go to **Practice file 1** on page 79.

9 **Work with a partner. Look at some profiles on a website. Student A, turn to file 01 on page 103. Student B, turn to file 29 on page 110.**

Practically speaking | How to spell

1 **05▷ Look at the letters of the alphabet. Listen and repeat. Why are the letters in these groups?**

1 A H J K
2 B C D E G P T V (Z)
3 F L M N S X (Z)
4 I Y
5 O
6 Q U W
7 R

2 **06▷ Listen to two conversations. Write the names.**

1 ______ 2 ______

3 **What is the question in each conversation?** ______

4 **Work with a partner. Say and spell**

- your name
- your company's name
- your job title.

Business communication | Saying hello and goodbye

1 **07▷ Two visitors are in Reception. Listen and complete this visitor board.**

> **FRIDAY 12TH SEPTEMBER**
>
> **Welcome today to:**
> **Mr Alek** ¹______
> **Ms** ²______ **Wozniak**
>
> **Visiting:**
> **Mrs** ³______ **Da Rocha**

2 **07▷ Match expressions 1–6 to responses a–f. Then listen and check.**

1 Hello. My name is Alek Gorski. ___
2 I'm Eva, Maria Da Rocha's assistant. ___
3 This is my assistant, Elzbieta Wozniak. ___
4 It's good to see you again. ___
5 How are you? ___
6 Do you know Elzbieta? ___

a Pleased to meet you, Eva.
b No. How do you do?
c How do you do, Mr Gorski?
d I'm fine.
e Nice to meet you.
f And you.

3 **Put expressions 1–6 and their responses into these categories.**

1 Saying hello and introducing yourself: *1c*, ___
2 Introducing someone: ___, ___
3 Saying hello to someone you know: ___, ___

4 **Work in groups of three. Practise this conversation.**

A Say hello to B (a colleague).

B Say hello to A (a colleague) and introduce C.

C Say hello to A (this is your first meeting).

Now change roles and practise the conversation again.

5 **Complete this conversation with the expressions in the list.**

Have a good journey   *See you soon*   *Nice meeting you*

Maria ¹________________, Alek.
Alek Yes, goodbye Maria.
Maria ²________________, Elzbieta.
Elzbieta Nice meeting you too.
Maria Bye. ³________________.
Alek Thanks. Bye.

6 **08▷ Listen and check. Then practise the conversation in 5 in your groups of three.**

» For more exercises, go to **Practice file 1** on page 78.

7 **Repeat the conversation in 4 and then say goodbye to A, B, or C.**

ⓘ » Interactive Workbook » **Email** and » **Exercises and Tests**

Key expressions

Saying hello and introducing yourself
Hello. My name is ... / I'm ...
Pleased to meet you.
How do you do?
Nice to meet you (too).

Introducing someone
This is ...
Do you know ...?

Saying hello to someone you know
It's good to see you again.
How are you?

Saying goodbye
Nice meeting you.
See you soon.
Have a good journey.
Goodbye / Bye.

ⓘ » Interactive Workbook
» **Phrasebank**

The introductions game

Play the introductions game with a partner.
Begin on START. Toss a coin.
Heads = move 1 square.
Tails = move 2 squares.
On a white square, follow the instruction.
On a blue square, respond.
The winner arrives on FINISH first.

FINISH 16	Tell your partner about your colleagues – names, jobs, nationalities. 15	Goodbye. 14	Introduce your partner to a customer. 13
Ask your partner: name? job? nationality? 9	Are you from Japan? 10	Introduce the person on card 11 to your partner. 11	Tell your partner about your boss – name, job, nationality. 12
Are you French? 8	Spell your company's name. 7	Hello, my name's Annie Da Silva. 6	Introduce yourself with the information on card 5. 5
START 1	Introduce yourself – give your name, job, and nationality. 2	Ask how your partner is. 3	How do you spell your name? 4

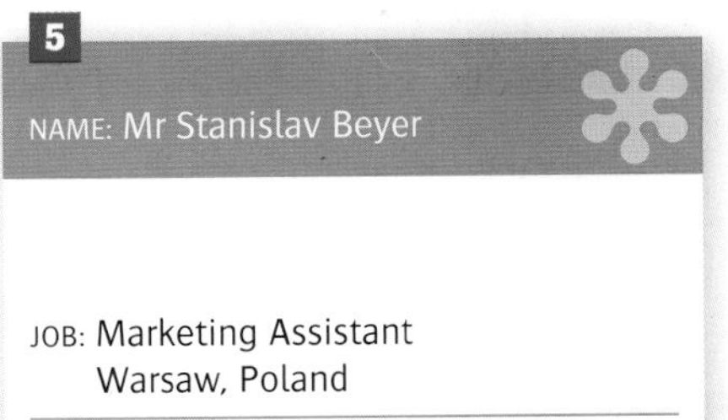

5
NAME: Mr Stanislav Beyer
JOB: Marketing Assistant
Warsaw, Poland

11
NAME: Ms Lesley Johnson
JOB: Technical Engineer
Middlesex, UK

Activity

2 | Products & services

Learning objectives in this unit

- Talking about company types and activities
- Asking about companies
- Saying numbers
- Booking and ordering by phone

Case study

- Choosing a supplier

Starting point

1 **What nationality are these companies: Lufthansa, Sony, Coca-Cola?**

2 **What do these companies produce: Philips, Bayer, Microsoft?**

3 **What do these companies provide: Banco do Brasil, Allianz Worldwide Care, CNN?**

Turn to file 55 on page 116 for the answers.

Working with words | Company types and activities

1 **Match these company types to the pictures.**

pharmaceuticals *real estate* *electronics* *recruitment*
hospitality *software* *financial services* *automobile*

1 ______

2 ______

3 ______

4 ______

5 ______

6 ______

7 ______

8 ______

2 **09▷ Listen to three people at a job fair. Which words do you hear from 1?**

3 **09▷ Listen again and complete these sentences.**

1 Natasha works for a [1] ______ company. She provides staff in the [2] ______ industry.
2 Malik's company produces [3] ______ for [4] ______ companies.
3 William works in [5] ______. He wants a job in the [6] ______ industry.

4 **10▷ Listen and underline the stress in these words.**

pharmaceuticals electronics recruitment hospitality
finance automobile

5 **What type of company is your company? What type of companies do you work with?**

6 **A company *produces* products and it *provides* services. Write *product* or *service* next to the words in C below.**

A	B	C
GlaxoSmithKline	provides	electronic equipment [1] *product*
Microsoft	produces	finance [2] ________
Sony		software [3] ________
Manpower		cars [4] ________
Toyota		staff [5] ________
Deutsche Bank AG		pharmaceuticals [6] ________

7 **Work with a partner. Take turns to make sentences about the companies in 6.**

Example: *Sony produces electronic equipment.*

8 **Does your company produce products or provide services? Or both?**

9 **11▷ Listen to a presentation about Kikkoman. Number the presentation slides 1 to 4 in the order you hear them.**

A ___

B ___

C ___

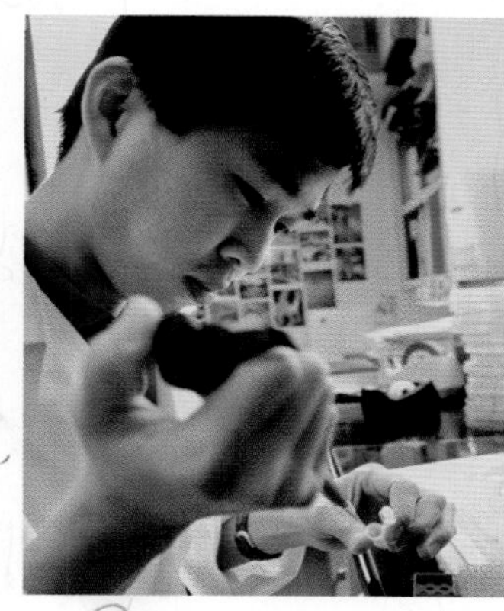
D ___

10 **Complete the presentation with these verbs.**

employ *sell* *export* *provide* *buy* *develop*

Kikkoman is a Japanese company and we [1] ________ 400 million litres of soy sauce every year. We [2] ________ 6,500 people in total. We [3] ________ soy sauce all over the world including Asia, North America, Australia, and Europe. We also [4] ________ new products for the pharmaceuticals industry. Restaurants, supermarkets, and Asian food shops [5] ________ our products and we also [6] ________ lessons in Japanese cooking – using Kikkoman products of course!

11 **11▷ Listen again and check your answers to 10.**

» For more exercises, go to **Practice file 2** on page 80.

12 **Prepare a presentation about your company. Use some of the sentences below.**

1 I'm ________
2 I'm from ________
3 I work for ________
4 We produce / provide ________
5 We employ ________
6 We develop ________
7 We export to ________
8 We sell our products to ________

13 **Now give your presentation to the class.**

ⓘ » Interactive Workbook » **Glossary**

Tip | *work* + preposition

We use the verb *work* in different ways:

work **for** (an employer / company): ***I work for** BMW.*

work **with** (people or another country): ***I work with** colleagues.*

work **in** (department or area of business): ***I work in** Production.*

Language at work | Present simple

1 CJ is a Korean company with different business areas. Match these business areas to the pictures below.

Bio Pharma *Home Shopping and Logistics*
Food and Food Service *Entertainment and Media*

A ____________________

We [1]*produce / produces* sugar and cooking oil. The company [2]*have / has* restaurants, cafes, and food shops. It [3]*provide / provides* meals for restaurants, schools, and hospitals.

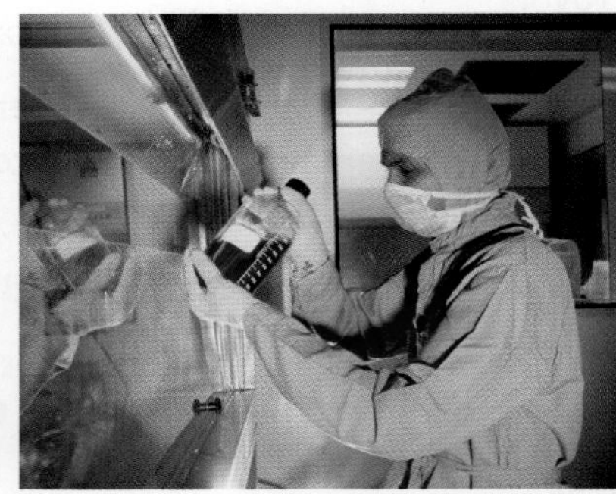

B ____________________

We [4]*export / exports* medicines to countries around the world. And we [5]*develop / develops* new biotechnological products.

C ____________________

The company [6]*produce / produces* films for the Korean market and abroad. We [7]*import / imports* films from foreign production companies ... and we [8]*have / has* eight cable TV channels ... and a chain of cinemas.

D ____________________

We [9]*provide / provides* a home shopping service. We [10]*have / has* a logistics centre. It [11]*provide / provides* transport and delivery services.

2 **12▷ Listen and <u>underline</u> the correct verb in *italics* in 1.**

3 The verbs in 1 are in the present simple tense. We use this tense for general facts. We add *-s* or *-es* to the verb after

1 I / you / we / they ☐ 2 he / she / it ☐

4 Work with a partner. Name a company from a business area in 1. Use the words in *italics* to talk about the company.

Example: *Canal Plus is a media company. It produces films for the European market.*

Tip | *have / has*

This verb is irregular.

have → *has* NOT ~~*haves*~~

5 13▷ **Listen and complete these questions and answers.**

1 **A** ________ ________ export these products?
  B Yes, we ________.
2 **A** ________ the ________ import films too?
  B Yes, ________ ________.
3 **A** ________ CJ provide financial services?
  B No, it ________ provide financial services.
4 **A** ________ you ________ medicines?
  B No, ________ ________. We export medicines.

Tip | short answers

In conversation, we answer questions with short answers. For example:

A *Do you export these products?*
B *Yes, we* ***do****.* NOT ~~*Yes, we export.*~~

6 **Complete these rules on the present simple tense.**

1 Make questions with the words ________ and ________.
2 Make negative sentences with the words ________ and ________.
3 Make positive short answers with *Yes, he* ________ / *Yes, I* ________.
4 Make negative short answers with *No, she* ________ / *No, we* ________.

» For more information and exercises, go to **Practice file 2** on page 81.

7 **Work with a partner. Ask and answer questions using the prompts below.**

Example: *A Do you work for an Italian company?*
B No, I don't. I work for a Brazilian company.

... you work for ...?
... your company export / import ...?
... your company produce / provide ...?
... your company develop / deliver ...?
... you have ...?
... your department employ ...?
... your customers buy ...?

Practically speaking | How to say numbers

1 **Can you say these numbers?**

2 14▷ **Listen and check.**

3 **Work with a partner. Answer these questions with numbers.**

1 What year is it?
2 What's your office telephone number and your mobile number?
3 What's the number of employees in your company?
4 What's the price of your company's main product or service?

Tip | Saying '0'

We say *oh* or *zero* for 0.

Business communication | Booking and ordering by phone

1 **Do you order products and services by telephone? What do you order?**

2 15▷ **A customer phones a restaurant. Who asks for 1–6? Listen and write *C* (customer) or *R* (restaurant manager)?**

1 a private room ___C___	4 a special price ___
2 a name ___	5 to confirm by email ___
3 the prices of set meals ___	6 an email address ___

3 15▷ **Listen again and complete these questions with verbs from the list.**

~~book~~ give confirm spell have (x2) repeat speak tell

1 Can I ___*book*___ a private room …?
2 Can you ______ me your name, please?
3 Can you ______ me the prices?
4 Can you ______ that, please?
5 Can I ______ a special price?
6 Can you ______ my booking by email?
7 Can I ______ your email address, please?
8 Can you ______ more slowly?
9 Can you ______ Hori?

4 16▷ **Listen to part of the conversation again. What words does the restaurant manager say after '*Yes*'? How does he say '*No*'?**

5 **Work with a partner. Take turns to ask and answer the questions in 3.**

» For more exercises, go to **Practice file 2** on page 80.

6 **Work with a partner. Make this conversation more polite, then practise it.**

A I want to order some mobile phones.
B What's the product code?
A DFK 1678.
B Slow down!
A DFK 1678.
B OK.
A I want delivery next week.
B We don't have them in stock.
A Send them as soon as possible.
B I want confirmation by email.
A What's your email address?
B info@bcom.biz.
A Spell it.
B info@bcom.biz
A Goodbye.

Key expressions

Requesting
Can I book / order …?

Asking for information
Can you give me …?
Can you tell me …?
Can you confirm …?

Responding
Yes, of course.
Sure.
Yes, we do.
I'm sorry, but we don't …

Asking for repetition and spelling
Can you repeat that?
Can you say that again?
Can you speak more slowly?
Can you spell that?

ⓘ » Interactive Workbook
» **Phrasebank**

7 **Work with a partner. Student A, turn to File 05 on page 104. Student B, turn to File 31 on page 110.**

ⓘ » Interactive Workbook » **Email** and » **Exercises and Tests**

Choosing a supplier

Background

Viking is an international offices supplies company. Read about the service it offers its clients.

Catalogue?	Yes
Free delivery?	Yes, for orders over £30, if ordered in same country Orders under £30 = £2.90 delivery charge
Return products?	Yes, within 30 days
International deliveries?	Yes and there's a website for each country
Delivery times?	Some areas, same day Other areas, next day

Discussion

1 **What do you think about the services Viking offers?**

2 **What is important for you when you order office supplies or other products?**
- free delivery?
- Internet ordering / ordering by phone?
- price?
- easy to return products?
- a catalogue to look at?

Task

You work for an international company in the Purchasing Department. It is important that the whole company has the same suppliers, so your job is to choose one which can provide products worldwide, is flexible, and has good prices.

1 17▷ **Listen to the phone call between a colleague and Euroffice and complete the information in the table.**

	Euroffice
Catalogue?	
Free delivery?	
Delivery times?	
Return products?	
International deliveries?	

2 **Work with a partner. Compare your information and discuss the differences between Viking and Euroffice. Which company do you want to choose as your new supplier? Why?**

3 **You want to buy a new desk for your office. Student A, turn to File 02 on page 103. Student B, turn to File 30 on page 110.**

Case study

3 | Location

Learning objectives in this unit

- Talking about your company location and buildings
- Asking for details about a workplace
- Starting and ending a telephone call
- Leaving telephone messages

Case study

- Finding the right location

Starting point

1. **Does your company have offices or operations in different countries? Where?**
2. **Do you always work in the same place? What places do you visit for your job?**
3. **Where is your head office?**

Working with words | Location and company buildings

1. **Read about Spectrum Brands. Is the company in different locations? Where?**

Spectrum Brands

Spectrum Brands is a global consumer products company. It produces batteries, lighting, and grooming products. It has a number of world-class brands, including Rayovac, Varta, and Remington. Spectrum Brands operates on six continents, it has about 10,000 employees, and it sells its products in around 120 countries.

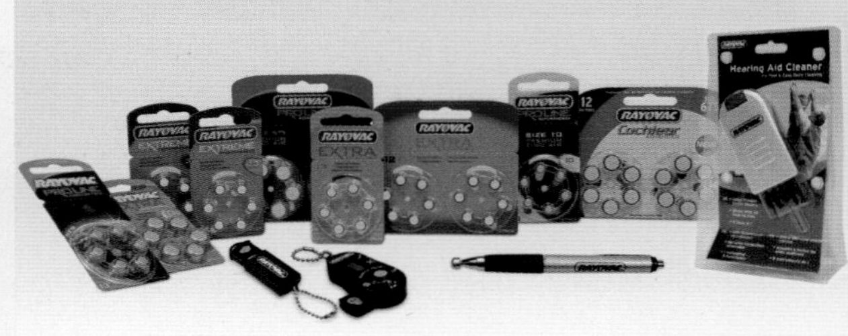

2. **Work with a partner. Take turns to ask each other to name countries in these continents and regions.**

   Example: *A Name two countries in the Middle East.*
   B Saudi Arabia and Dubai.

the Middle East ___	North America ___	Latin America ___
Asia-Pacific ___	Africa ___	Europe ___

3. **18▷ Listen to a presentation about Spectrum Brands. Number the continents and regions in 2 in the order you hear them.**

Tip | *about, around*

about / *around* = not exactly

The company has 847 employees = The company has ***about 850*** *employees.*

It sells products in 102 countries = It sells products in ***around 100*** *countries.*

4 18▷ **Listen again and write numbers and locations in the notes below.**

WORKPLACE	WHERE
Head office	Atlanta, USA
Technical centre	Madison, Wisconsin
Factories	twenty-one in [1]__________
	four in [2]__________ (Guatemala, Brazil, Colombia)
	two in [3]__________ (Germany, UK)
	one in [4]__________
Sales offices	[5]__________ in North America
	[6]__________ in Latin America
	[7]__________ in Asia-Pacific
	[8]__________ in Europe
	One in Dubai for the [9]__________ and Africa
Distribution centres	[10]__________ around the world

5 **Match the five workplaces in 4 to these pictures.**

1 ________________

2 ________________

3 ________________

4 ________________

5 ________________

6 **Work with a partner. Read sentences 1–5. Which workplace from 5 do they describe?**

1 We make all our products here.
2 This is where we do our research and development.
3 Our sales reps visit customers four days a week, but come here on Fridays.
4 The Managing Director and all the other company directors work here.
5 The products come here and we deliver them to customers.

» For more exercises, go to **Practice file 3** on page 82.

7 **What is your workplace? What do you do there? Tell the class.**

8 **Prepare a presentation about your company or use the information about the company in File 03 on page 103. Write notes about the workplaces and the locations.**

9 **Give your presentation to your partner or to the class. Use some of these expressions.**

Good morning. Today, I'd like to tell you about ...
We are ... / We have ...

ⓘ » Interactive Workbook » **Glossary**

Language at work | *There is / are* | *Some / any*

1 Read about Dubai. Is it a good location for business? Why?

Why do more businesses choose Dubai?

LOCATION

Dubai is at the centre of the Middle East and the city is the perfect meeting place for the markets of Europe, Asia, and Africa. There are over 65 airlines to 100 destinations worldwide from our international airport.

BUSINESS

Dubai is the perfect location for a regional office and has conference and exhibition centres. There are some excellent services (banks, law firms, advertising agencies) and hotels at every price.

TRANSPORT

Unlike many cosmopolitan cities, there isn't a problem with transport in Dubai. Take a taxi or use public transport – there's a bus every 20 minutes on most bus routes.

2 Complete these sentences.

1 Use *there is* / ________ in positive sentences.
2 Use ________ / *there aren't* in negative sentences.
3 Complete this table for questions and short answers.

Questions	Short answers
Is there ...?	*Yes,* ________. / *No, there isn't.*
Are there ...?	*Yes, there are.* / *No,* ________.

3 19▷ Two people are discussing Dubai as the location for a large conference. Complete their conversation with words from the list. Then listen and check your answers.

there are   *there is*   *there isn't*   *is there*   *are there*

A Dubai is a great location for a conference. The weather is always good.
B What about the airport? [1] ARE THERE lots of international flights?
A Yes, [2] THERE ARE. And [3] THERE ISN'T a problem with transport from the airport because public transport is excellent in Dubai.
B But [4] IS THERE a good place for a conference?
A Yes, [5] THERE IS. It's the Dubai International Exhibition and Convention complex. It's perfect.

4 Read these sentences. When do we use *some*? When do we use *any*?

There's a taxi.
*There are **some** taxis.*
*There aren't **any** taxis.*
*Are there **any** taxis?*
Is there a taxi?

5 Work with a partner. Ask and answer questions about your place of work.

Example: ***A*** *Is there a car park for staff?*
B *Yes, there is.*

In the company	Near the company
car park for staff	good restaurants
canteen	airport
drinks machines	shops
conference room	gym

» For more information and exercises, go to **Practice file 3** on page 83.

6 **Work with a partner. You want information about hotels in Dubai for a meeting. Student A, turn to File 06 on page 104. Student B, ask Student A about The Arabian Garden Hotel. Write notes in the table below.**

Example: *Is there a bus to the airport?*

	The Arabian Garden Hotel	The Dubai Grand Hotel
Bus to the airport?		
Car park?		
Restaurants and bars?		
Leisure facilities (swimming pool, gym)?		
Services (Internet, bank)?		
Conference / Meeting rooms?		
Other services?		

7 **Now repeat the exercise in 6. Student A, ask Student B about The Dubai Grand Hotel and write notes in the table. Student B, turn to File 32 on page 110.**

8 **Now compare the two hotels and choose one for a conference. Then present your reasons to another pair.**

Example: *At the Arabian Garden Hotel, there's a ..., but there aren't any ...*

Practically speaking | How to start and end a telephone call

1 **Read these expressions for the telephone. Are they at the start or the end? Who says them? The caller, the receiver, or both?**

	start / end	caller / receiver
1 Hello, the Dubai Grand hotel.		
2 Can I help you?		
3 This is ...		
4 I'm calling about ...		
5 Thanks for your help.		
6 You're welcome.		
7 Goodbye.		

2 20▷ **Listen to two parts of a telephone call. Check your answers in 1.**

3 **Work with a partner. Take turns to be the caller and hotel representative. Telephone a hotel about**

- business services (meeting rooms, Internet access, fax)
- car parking and car hire
- rooms for 30 people next week
- buses from the airport.

Tip | *This is ...*

On the telephone say your name like this:

This is *Raymond Sadler.*
My name's *Raymond Sadler.*
It's *Raymond Sadler.*
NOT ~~*I am Raymond Sadler.*~~

Business communication | Leaving telephone messages

1 21▷ **Listen to parts of two telephone calls. What mistakes does the receiver make?**

2 21▷ **Listen again. How do the callers correct the information?**

1 ______________________________

2 ______________________________

3 **Work with a partner. Telephone your partner and check and correct details. Student A, turn to File 04 on page 103. Student B, turn to File 37 on page 112.**

4 22▷ **Listen to a telephone conversation. Complete the message.**

MESSAGE FOR: Teresa Baum

FROM: MRS ANDAC

CALLING ABOUT: METTING

PHONE NUMBER: 00442073996344

CALL BACK? ☒ **URGENT?** ☐

5 22▷ **Match 1–9 to a–i. Then listen again and check.**

1	Could I speak ___	a	… your message.
2	I'm sorry, but ___	b	… a contact number?
3	Could I leave ___	c	… a message for her?
4	It's ___	d	… right?
5	So ___	e	… that's A-N-D-A-C.
6	Can she call ___	f	… to Teresa Baum, please?
7	Can I have ___	g	… Richard Andac.
8	Is that ___	h	… she isn't here this morning.
9	I'll give her ___	i	… me back as soon as possible?

» For more exercises, go to **Practice file 3** on page 82.

6 **Work with a partner. Practise leaving messages. Student A, turn to file 07 on page 104. Student B, turn to file 34 on page 111.**

ⓘ » Interactive Workbook » **Email** and » **Exercises and Tests**

Key expressions

Asking to speak to someone
Could I speak to …?
I'd like to speak to …
Is … there?

Leaving a message
Could I leave a message?
My number is …
Can she call me back (as soon as possible)?

Take a message
I'm sorry, but she isn't here / available.
Can I take a message?
Can I have a contact number?
I'll give him / her your message.

Checking details
So that's …
Is that right?

Correcting details
No, it's N as in New York / O as in Oslo.

ⓘ » Interactive Workbook
» **Phrasebank**

Finding the right location

Background

Best place for your business?

Martin Bloemberg, a location expert, says it's very important to get information about the location for your business. You must find out:

- are there other businesses in the area with the same product?
- are there a lot of people living near your business?
- is there car parking?
- is there public transport nearby?

Before you find a location you need to ask local people about the area. If you don't do this, you could lose a lot of money!

Discussion

1 **What must you find out about the area before you buy an office or shop?**

2 **Why?**

3 **Where's your company? Is it in a good location for customers / staff / business?**

Task

You have a sandwich bar in your town. Business is good. You want to open another sandwich bar, but you don't know where. You have contacts in three other towns. They have information about three sandwich bars for sale in these towns.

1 **Work in groups of three. Read about one of the locations. Student A, turn to File 08 on page 104. Student B, turn to File 35 on page 111. Student C, turn to File 56 on page 116.**

2 **Take turns to present your location to your group. While you listen to other members of your group, complete the table for their locations.**

3 **In your groups, choose one location for your sandwich bar.**

Case study

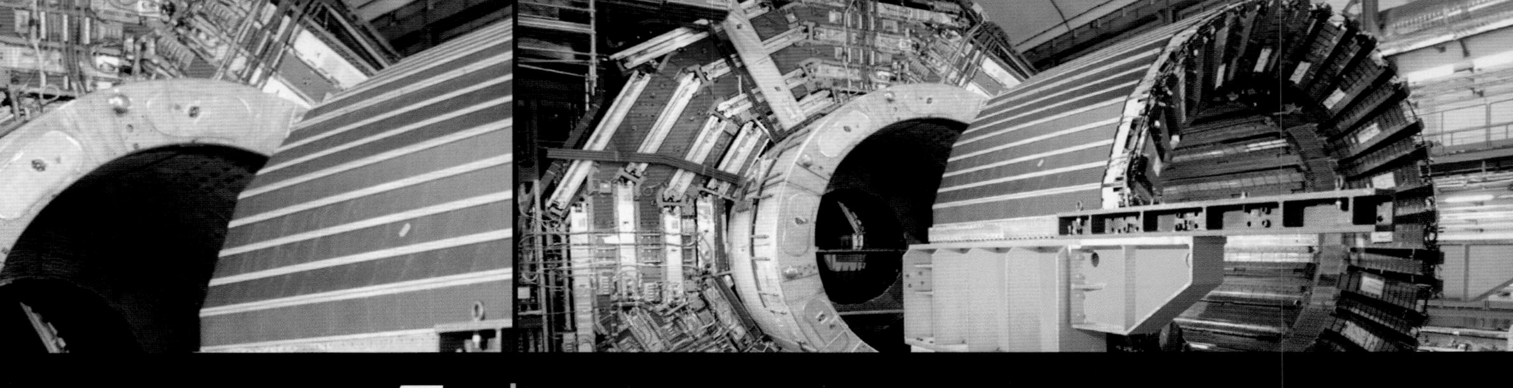

4 | Technology

Learning objectives in this unit

- Talking about technology
- Talking about everyday activities
- Asking questions
- Sequencing actions
- Asking for and offering help

Case study

- Making use of technology

Starting point

What technology do you use

- for work?
- in your private life?

Compare your answers with the class.

Working with words | Technology and functions

1 **Read this text about Virgin. What services does it offer customers?**

What's new with Virgin?

Fast Ticket Machines
Save time and get your tickets from the new Fast Ticket Machines at many stations.

Use of electronic devices
Why fly? On the train you never switch off electronic devices for take-off or landing. Each seat has power points for laptops and you can recharge your mobile phone.

First class waiting areas
Now at all large stations, first class travellers can use the business waiting areas with desks and photocopiers. Meet clients here and use the wireless Internet connection to check emails.

2 **Match words from the text in 1 to these pictures.**

1 FAST TICKETS

3 Mobile phone

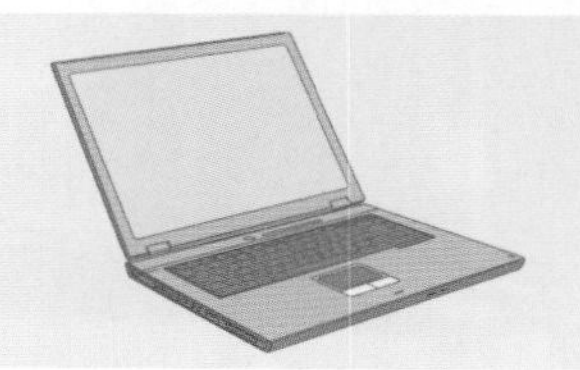

2 laptops

4 WIRELESS INTERNET

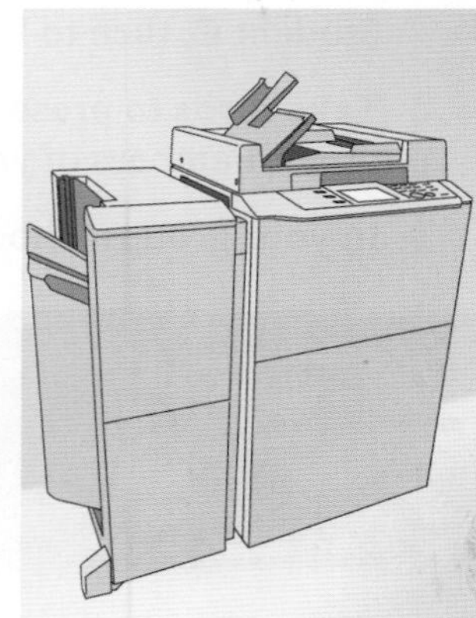

5 PHOTOCOPIERS

3 **23▷ Listen and match the technology in 2 to these conversations.**

1 TICKETS MACHINE
2 MOBILE PHONE
3 WIRELESS CONNECTIONS
4 PHOTOCOPIERS

4 23▷ **Listen again and match the words in the list to 1–5 below.**

battery *screen* *button* *start menu* *username and password*

1 ticket machine ________ 4 Internet ________
2 mobile phone ________ 5 photocopier ________
3 laptop ________

5 **Work with a partner. Think of two types of technology or machine. Write definitions. Read them to your partner. Guess the technology.**

Example: *A* *You call people with it.*
B *A mobile phone?*
A *Correct!*

6 **Technology words are often the same or similar in different languages. Are the words in 4 similar in your language? What about other technology words?**

7 **Read audio script 23 on page 120. Underline the technology-related verb + noun combinations. Then write the verbs below.**

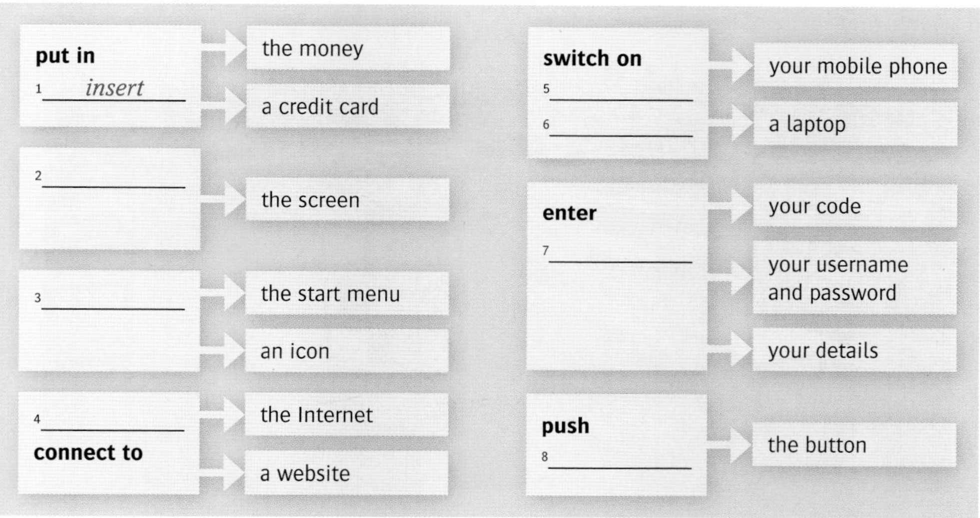

» For more exercises, go to **Practice file 4** on page 84.

8 **Look at these actions. Make verb + noun combinations about each picture.**

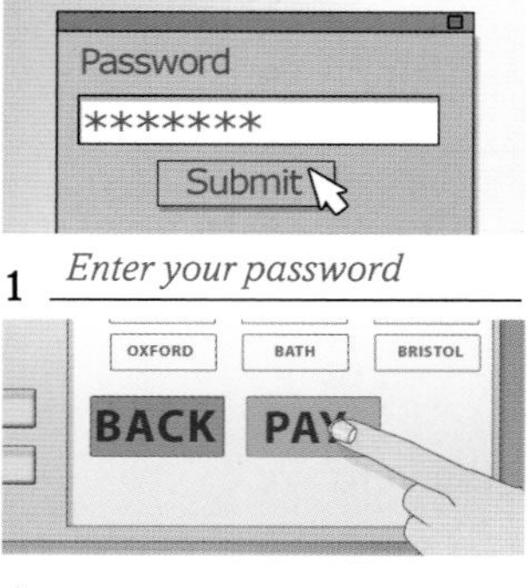

1 *Enter your password*

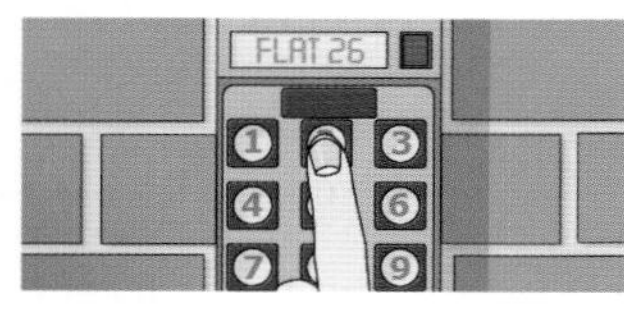

2 ________

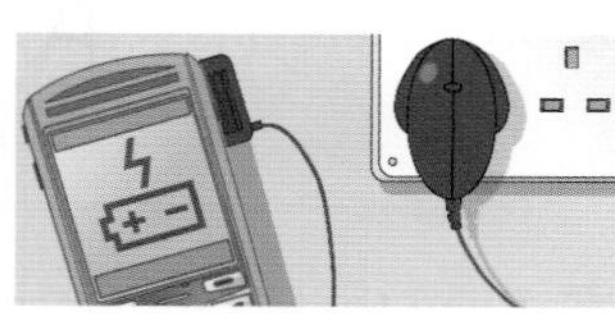

3 ________

4 ________

5 ________

6 ________

9 **Tick (✓) the actions in 8 you do at work. Tell your partner when you do them.**

Example: *I enter my password when I switch on my computer.*

ⓘ » Interactive Workbook » **Glossary**

Tip | Phrasal verbs

A phrasal verb has a main verb + particle: *put in, switch on, log on.*

Some phrasal verbs can change position:

Put *the money* ***in***. / ***Put in*** *the money.*
Switch *the phone* ***on***. / ***Switch on*** *the phone.*

Some can't change position:

Click on *the icon.* NOT ~~*Click the icon on.*~~

Language at work | Adverbs of frequency | Questions

1 **Do you work eight hours a day? How many hours a week?**

2 **Read this article and answer these questions.**

1 Do they work eight hours a day?
2 Do they arrive on time?
3 Do they take breaks?

The Super employees!

How often do you work 9 or 10 hours a day? Well, imagine these workers: They **always** work 16 hours a day, seven days a week. They are **never** late for work because they **never** leave the building. They **rarely** take breaks – only to recharge their batteries. Of course, they aren't human, they're robots.

So where do these robots work? Staples – the US office product distributor – employs them in its warehouse in Chambersburg, Pennsylvania. 50% of staff are robots who move items around the warehouse. Because the new 'employees' are so good, Staples wants more in its other 29 warehouses.

3 **Does your company use robots? If not, do you have jobs for a robot in your place of work?**

4 **Complete this scale with the adverbs in bold in 2.**

1 ________ 2 ________ sometimes often usually 3 ________

0% ●———— 50% ————● 100%

5 **Read these sentences then underline the correct word in *italics* in 1–2.**

They always work 16 hours a day.
They rarely take breaks.
They are never late.

1 With all verbs except *be*, the adverb goes *before / after* the verb.
2 With *be*, the adverb goes *before / after* the verb.

6 **Make true sentences about you. Use an adverb of frequency.**

Example: *often*
I ^ work ten hours a day.

1 I work ten hours a day.
2 I'm late for work.
3 I take breaks.
4 I work five days a week.
5 I'm sick and take a day off.

7 **Work with a partner. Ask and answer questions about the sentences in 6. Use an adverb in your answer.**

Example: *A Do you work 10 hours a day?*
B No, I never work 10 hours a day. I work ...

8 **Find two questions in the article in 2. What are the question words?**

9 **Match questions 1–7 to answers a–g.**

1 **Who** do the robots work for? ___
2 **What** does Staples deliver? ___
3 **Where** do the robots work? ___
4 **How often** do they take a day off? ___
5 **When** do they stop work? ___
6 **Why** do they stop work? ___
7 **How** does Staples use the robots? ___

a Office products.
b After 16 hours.
c To recharge their batteries.
d To move items.
e Never.
f In the warehouse.
g For Staples.

10 **What do the question words in bold in 9 refer to?**

1 The way / method *How*
2 General information *What*
3 Time ________
4 People ________
5 Places ________
6 Reasons ________
7 Frequency ________

» For more information and exercises, go to **Practice file 4** on page 85.

11 **Work with a partner. Ask and answer questions about your company and your work. Use these prompts.**

Who / work for?
What / produce or provide?
Where / work?
Why / like / your job?
When / start / work?
How often / take / day off?

Practically speaking | How to use sequencing words

1 **24▷ Listen to how the robots at Staples do their job. Put these stages in order.**

a 4 the person takes the correct items for the order.
b 1 the warehouse computer receives customer orders.
c 5 the robot returns the box and starts again.
d 3 the robot finds the box and delivers it to a human co-worker.
e 2 the computer tells a robot to find the correct box.

2 **24▷ Listen again and match these words to the five stages.**

Example: *First of all, the warehouse computer receives customer orders.*

first of all ___ finally ___ after that ___ then ___ next ___

3 **Think of stages for a process at work or your typical day. Tell your partner the stages with the sequencing words in 2.**

Example: *First of all, I check emails. Then, I send new orders to the warehouse. Next, I ...*

Business communication | Asking for and offering help

1 What is the difference between the Internet and Intranet? Does your company have an Intranet?

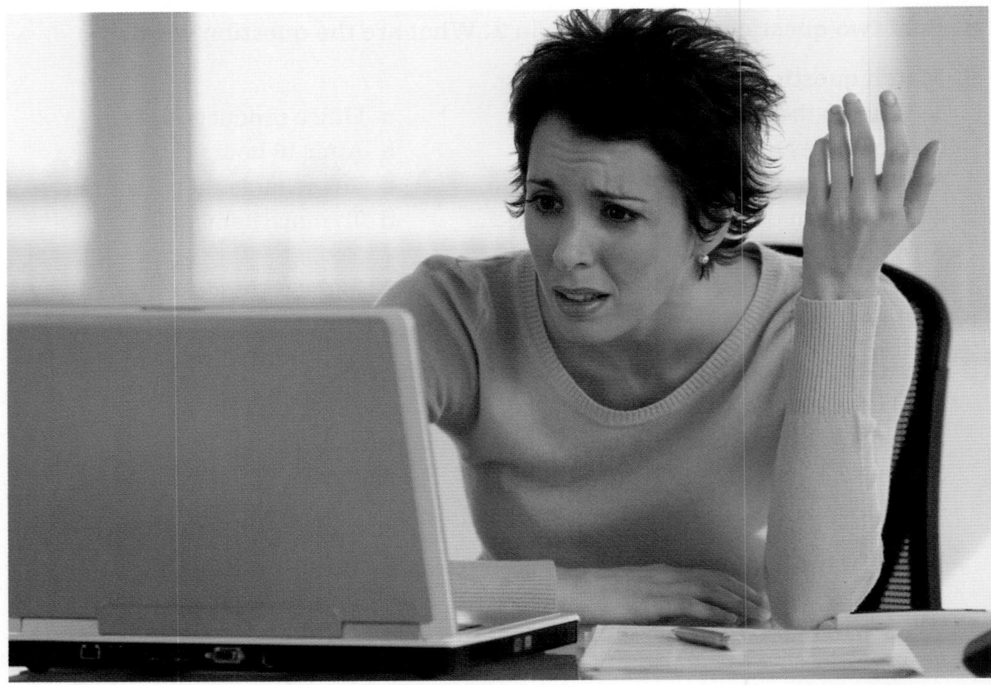

2 25▷ Listen to two colleagues, Chen and Magda. Underline the correct answer in *italics*.

1 Magda can't use the *Internet / Intranet.*
2 You need to enter the password with *lower case letters / UPPER CASE LETTERS.*
3 The Intranet gives company *news / products.*
4 You can send messages to *colleagues / clients.*
5 Magda can't *log out of the Intranet / switch the computer off.*

3 Are these expressions asking for help (*A*), offering help (*O*), or responding (*R*)?

1 Can you help me? __
2 Sure. __
3 How do I ...? __
4 I'm trying to ... __
5 Do you want a hand? __
6 That would be good. __

4 25▷ Listen again and check your answers to 3.

» For more exercises, go to **Practice file 4** on page 84.

5 Work with a partner. Student A, turn to File 10 on page 105. Student B, turn to File 41 on page 113.

6 You have a list of technical problems below. Move around the class and ask different people for help. Find someone who can help you to

- log on to your company's website
- set the alarm clock on your mobile phone
- get a coffee from the machine in the corridor
- install a printer to your computer
- buy a train ticket from the machines at your local station.

ⓘ » Interactive Workbook » **Email** and » **Exercises and Tests**

Key expressions

Asking for help
Can you help me?
Can you give me a hand?
How do I ...?
I'm trying to ...
I don't know how to ...

Responding to a request for help
Yes, of course.
Sure.

Offering help
Can I help?
Do you want a hand?

Responding to offers
Yes, please.
That would be good.

ⓘ » Interactive Workbook
» **Phrasebank**

Making use of technology

Background

1 Look at these pictures. What are they and what are they used for?

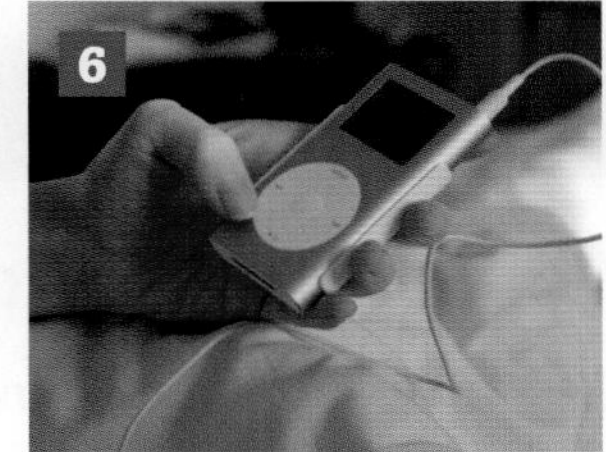

2 26▷ Listen to two people explain how they use two of the items of technology in 1. What items are they talking about?

3 Can you think of any unusual uses for the other technology in 1?

Discussion

1 Which of the products do you use? Which product is not useful for you? Mark each product on the line.

Useful ———————————————— Not useful

2 Work with a partner and discuss your ranking.

3 Work in small groups. Re-order your ranking for your group. Which is your group's favourite product?

Task

1 Work in small groups and think of a new product / new technology that can make your lives better, or a new use for a product. What is it? How does it work?

2 Present your idea to the rest of the class. While you listen to the other presentations, prepare two questions to ask about the products.

3 Which idea was your favourite?

Case study

5 | Communication

Learning objectives in this unit
- Dealing with documents and correspondence
- Talking about a past event
- Checking actions
- Apologizing
- Solving problems

Case study
- Everyday tasks

Starting point

1 **What types of correspondence do you use in your job?**

2 **How many hours a day do you spend on correspondence and paperwork?**

Working with words | Documents and correspondence

1 **Fujitsu provides IT and communications solutions. Read about its work with three companies.**

1 What product or system does each company use?
2 What is the result?

Three ways FUJITSU helps clients to reduce paperwork and improve communication:

The nurses at PinnacleHealth use Fujitsu's pen tablets for patient information. They never print a **hard copy** so now they have more time for patients.

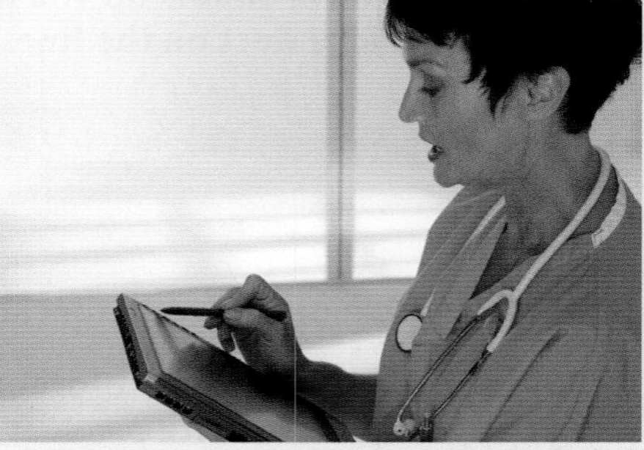

The recruitment firm, Spring Personnel, receives hundreds of **CV**s, letters, and **business cards**. But with the Fujitsu ScanSnap, the company can scan and save them electronically. It reduces 'paper filed in the office by 90%', says Lucy Taylor, branch co-ordinator.

The global delivery company, TNT, deals with 30,000 items every day. In 2002, each item needed 4 pieces of paperwork including an **order form** from the customer, an **invoice** to bill the customer, and a **delivery note** and **receipt** for when the item was delivered. Working with Fujitsu, TNT now has an electronic system called PACS. It reduces delivery times by up to 8 hours.

2 **Does your company produce lots of paperwork? How does it reduce it?**

3 **What documents do you need in these situations? Match the words in bold in 1.**

1 You want to apply for a job. ________________
2 You want to place an order. ________________
3 You make a payment. ________________
4 You meet someone for the first time. ________________
5 You send a customer a list of the items they ordered and the total price. ________________
6 The delivery company brings you 20 boxes. ________________
7 Your boss wants to read your report. You need to print it. ________________

4 **Which of the documents in 3 do you use at work? What other types of documents do you deal with at work?**

5 **27▷ Listen to a telephone conversation.**

1 What is the problem?
2 What types of documents or correspondence do they mention?

6 **27▷ Listen again and make verb + noun combinations from A and B. Then match the words to the pictures.**

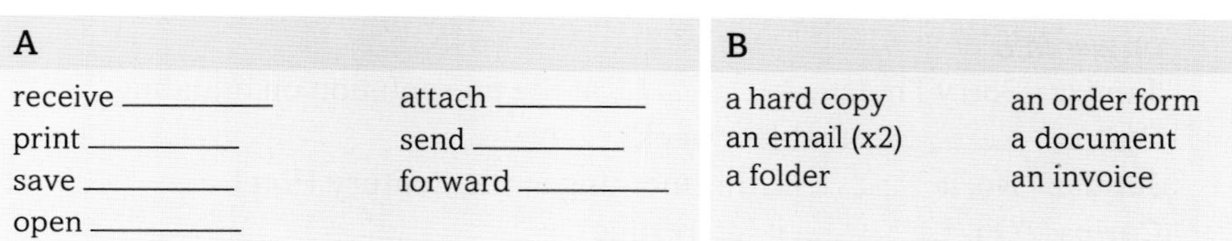

A		B	
receive ________	attach ________	a hard copy	an order form
print ________	send ________	an email (x2)	a document
save ________	forward ________	a folder	an invoice
open ________			

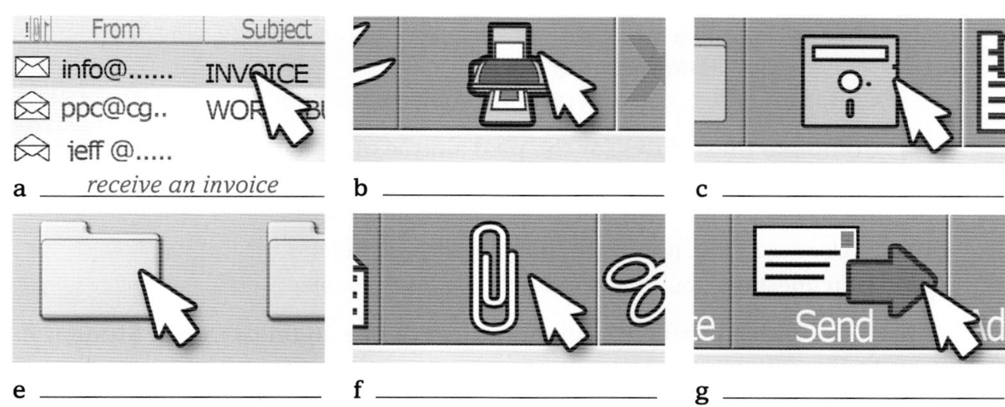

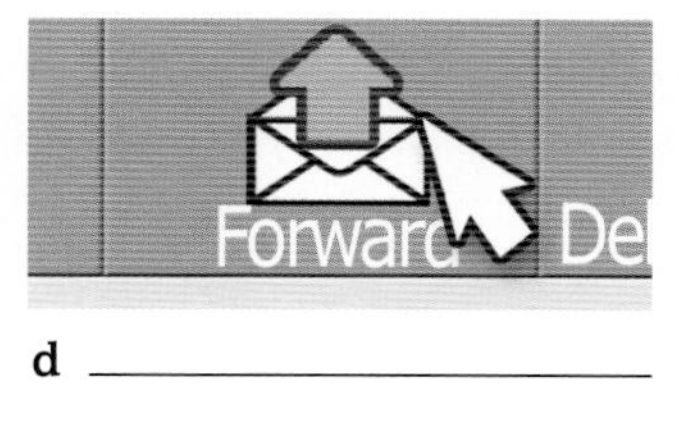

a *receive an invoice* b ________ c ________ d ________
e ________ f ________ g ________

7 **What other verb + noun combinations can you make from 3 and 6?**

Example: *receive / print / save / open / send / forward an email.*

» For more exercises, go to **Practice file 5** on page 86.

8 **Work with a partner. Student A, turn to file 09 on page 105. Student B, turn to file 36 on page 111.**

9 **Work in small groups. Discuss these questions.**

1 Do you write letters at work or do you always write emails?
2 How many emails do you receive a day at work? Are they always necessary?
3 Do you prefer to telephone or email to:
- arrange to meet?
- solve a problem?
- find out information?

ⓘ » Interactive Workbook » **Glossary**

Language at work | Past simple: *be* and regular verbs

1 **Do you ever have meetings at breakfast? Do you think this is a good time for meetings or presentations?**

2 28▷ **Listen to a conversation between Janusz and Carlos and underline the correct words in *italics*.**

ALPHA MARKETING CONSULTANTS

Alpha Marketing Consultants welcomes you to a [1]*presentation / meeting*:

'Sobieski on Brands: The Branding of Eastern Europe'

VENUE:
The Century [2]*Restaurant / Hotel*
SPEAKER:
Maike Sobieski
Buffet [3]*breakfast / lunch* starts at 7.30. Presentation at 8.15.

3 28▷ **Listen again and complete the conversation with *was, wasn't, were,* or *weren't*.**

Janusz Sorry I'm late. I [1]________ at the presentation on branding.
Carlos [2]________ that last week?
Janusz No, it [3]________ this morning at the Century Hotel.
Carlos Oh. [4]________ it interesting?
Janusz Yes, it [5]________, and there [6]________ lots of good questions at the end. The breakfast [7]________ good too! Anyway, why [8]________ you in the office yesterday?
Carlos There [9]________ terrible problems with flights from Rome, so I …

4 **Complete these rules for the past simple of *be* with *was, were, wasn't,* or *weren't*.**

1 Use ________ or ________ in positive sentences.
2 Use ________ or ________ in negative sentences.
3 In questions, put the verb *before / after* the subject.

5 **Work with a partner. Student A, turn to File 16 on page 107. Student B, turn to File 38 on page 112.**

6 **Read the two emails below.**

1 When was the meeting?
2 What was the reason for the meeting?
3 Why didn't Piotr organize the next business breakfast?

Subject: Next month's business event

Hi Piotr
Sorry I wasn't at the meeting last Monday. What **did** you **decide** to do about next month's business event?
Lydia
Alpha Marketing

Hi Lydia
We **decided** to ask the management expert, Ron Peters, to give the next presentation on 25th.
I'm afraid I **didn't have** time to email Mr Peters or book the hotel last week and now I'm away for a week.
Can you organize it? Thank you.
Piotr

Tip | *was not / wasn't*

When speaking, use *wasn't / weren't*:
*I **wasn't** at the meeting.*

In formal or written English, use *was not / were not*:
*The company **was not** able to invest.*

7 **Look at the verbs in bold in 6 and complete these rules about the past simple.**

1 Make positive sentences with verb + ________ .
2 Make negative sentences with ________ + verb.
3 For questions and short answers, use ________ / *didn't*.

8 29▷ **Lydia telephones Piotr about the presentation. Listen and tick (✓) what Lydia did on this 'to do' list.**

To do:
Call Ron Peters
Confirm the time of the presentation
Telephone 'Century Hotel'
Book the room

9 29▷ **Listen again and complete these sentences using the past simple of the verbs in brackets.**

1 I just ________ to check ... (want)
2 ... if you ________ Ron Peters. (call)
3 What ________ he ________? (say)
4 Why ________ he ________ to speak then? (not / want)
5 I ________ the Century Hotel. (telephone)
6 ________ you ________ it? (book)
No, I ________. (not / do)

» For more information and exercises, go to **Practice file 5** on page 87.

10 30▷ **Sometimes the *-ed* adds an extra syllable to the verb. Listen and write the number of syllables in each verb.**

1 decide *2* – decided *3*
2 telephone ___ – telephoned ___
3 want ___ – wanted ___
4 call ___ – called ___
5 invite ___ – invited ___

11 **Work with a partner. Student A, turn to File 11 on page 105. Student B, turn to File 39 on page 112.**

12 **Work with a partner. Ask and answer these questions.**

- When was your last meeting?
- Where was it?
- What did you talk about?
- Was it interesting?
- Were many people there? Who were they?
- Were there lots of questions?
- What did you decide?

Practically speaking | How to apologize

1 31▷ **Listen to three conversations.**

1 How does the speaker apologize?
2 What reason does the speaker give?

2 **Work with a partner. Take turns to apologize in these situations and give a reason.**

- you're late for a job interview
- you didn't book the hotel for your boss
- you weren't at the department meeting this morning
- you didn't remember your colleague's birthday
- a customer didn't receive a delivery

Business communication | Solving problems

1 **Do you have these problems at work? Who normally solves them?**

- late deliveries
- bad products or services
- machinery or equipment not working
- human mistakes
- angry customers

2 **32▷ Listen to a telephone conversation. Which problems in 1 do they have?**

3 **32▷ Listen again and complete the conversation.**

1 ... we ________ a problem with the order for Gosport.
2 We ________ all the baseball bats and T-shirts yesterday, so I ________ ship them tomorrow. But the logos on the caps ________.
3 We ________ fix the machine today and print them again.
4 OK. ________ worry.
5 I know the Purchasing Manager at Gosport, so I ________ to him ...
6 We ________ give another delivery date for this.
7 Sure. I ________ the factory now and I ________ you know as soon as I can.
8 That ________ be great. Thanks a lot.

» For more exercises, go to **Practice file 5** on page 86.

4 **Work with a partner. Read this email from your boss.**

Dear both
I'm in meetings all day today so can you deal with these between you, please?
- who is on Reception this week? (where's Astrid?)
- Gosport telephoned. Purchasing says the invoice was wrong for the last order.
- the new printers don't work with our computers. What can IT do about it?
- did someone book my tickets for Moscow? Remember I go next Monday.
- Ellen in Sales leaves this week. Can we organize a leaving party on Friday? And a present?

Now turn to your information files. Student A, turn to File 12 on page 105. Student B, turn to File 40 on page 112.

5 **Think of a problem at work this week. Explain it to your partner. Take turns to try and solve your partner's problem and promise action.**

» Interactive Workbook » **Email** and » **Exercises and Tests**

Key expressions

Explaining the problem
I've / We've got a problem with ...
There are some problems with ...
I / We can't ...
We did X ..., but Y didn't work ...

Solving the problem
You / We need to ...
We can ...

Promising action
I'll ... (speak to ... / explain the situation / call ... / let you know as soon as I can)

Responding and thanking
Don't worry.
That would be great.
Thanks a lot for your help.
No problem.

» Interactive Workbook
» **Phrasebank**

Everyday tasks

Background

Tasks Everyday – get your tasks done
Tasks Everyday offers virtual office assistants to other companies to help with any task that can be done by phone or email, for example, making appointments or booking flights. The assistants work every day, 24 hours a day, and provide a personal service to the company that uses them. Some companies use them all the time; other companies use them during staff holidays.

Discussion

1. **Where do the office assistants for Tasks Everyday work?**
2. **Do you like this idea for your company?**
3. **What problems can you see with this service?**

Task

You work for Tasks Everyday. Your client, Nina, is an administrator for Balfour Furnishings and is on holiday for two weeks, so all of her emails and phone calls are re-directed to you. It is the 15th February.

BALFOUR FURNISHINGS – ORDER FORM

CLIENT NAME: OMEGA **ACCOUNT NUMBER:** OG6548791 **DATE:** 31 JAN

Item code	Price	Quantity	Total

What's the order?

We want to book a meeting room for an international meeting: 2nd April.
Please contact us: Human Resources in Budapest, and confirm the booking.
Thanks

Confirmation of your flight details:

Booking reference 02687986P
Ms K Adams
Frankfurt to Hong Kong
Flight number LH738
4th March
Depart 17.45
Arrive 10.30

PLEASE PRINT THIS OFF AND KEEP AS YOUR RECEIPT.

PHONE MESSAGE
NAME: Tony
TIME: 7.30 a.m., 15/02
MESSAGE: At Milan airport. Plane is cancelled. Can't get to meeting this afternoon in London. Please find someone else to go.

1. **Work with a partner. Talk about the items above and decide what you need to do with each one.**
2. **Now decide on the two jobs you need to do first.**
3. **Make two phone calls. Student A, turn to File 13 on page 105. Student B, turn to File 42 on page 113.**

6 Contacts

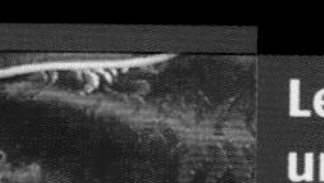

Learning objectives in this unit

- Talking about food and drink
- Ordering food in a restaurant or café
- Talking about the past with time expressions
- Describing a trip
- Making conversation

Activity

- The socializing game

Starting point

1 **Does your company have many visitors? Where do they have lunch? Where do they go in the evening? For dinner? To the theatre?**

2 **Do you visit other companies? How do they entertain you?**

Working with words | Food and drink

1 **Work with a partner. Read this article and discuss the questions for:**
1 your own country
2 other countries you visit

Tips for Travellers: Eating Out

In many countries, the restaurant – not the office – is the real place for business. So make sure you can answer these questions before your next trip abroad.

1 What do you eat for lunch or dinner in your country?
2 Are there any special or local dishes?
3 Is it normal to drink alcohol?
4 How many courses are there?
5 Who pays the bill?
6 What is the tip in most restaurants? 0%? 10%? 20%?

2 33▷ **Listen to two people at a restaurant. What do they order? What is their total bill?**

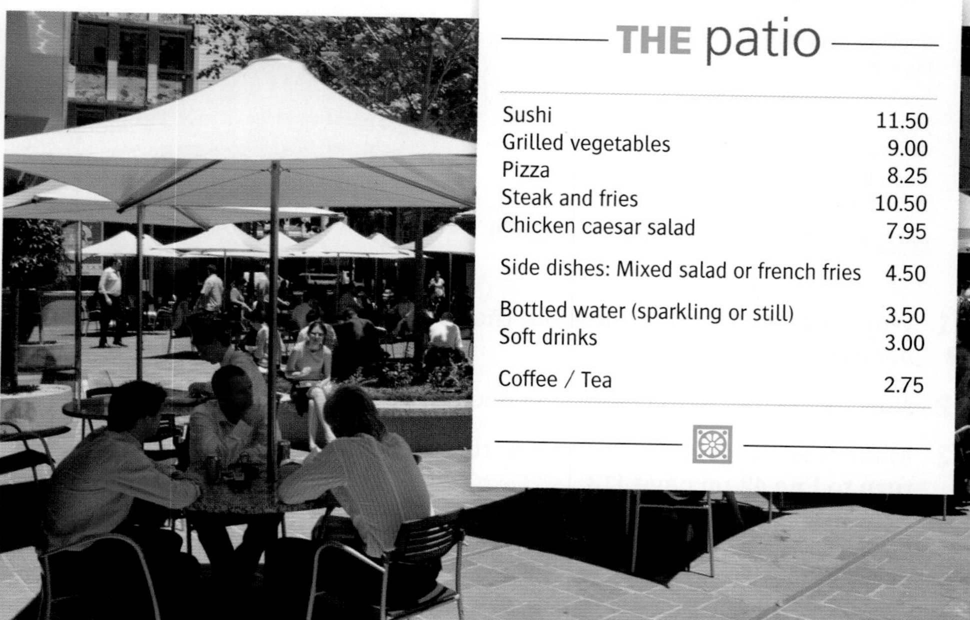

THE patio

Sushi	11.50
Grilled vegetables	9.00
Pizza	8.25
Steak and fries	10.50
Chicken caesar salad	7.95
Side dishes: Mixed salad or french fries	4.50
Bottled water (sparkling or still)	3.50
Soft drinks	3.00
Coffee / Tea	2.75

3 33▷ **Listen again and underline the correct words in *italics*.**

1 *Would* / *Do* you like sushi?
2 *We like* / *We'd like* a bottle of sparkling water.
3 *Do you like* / *Would you like* to order first?
4 *I'd* / *I'll* have the grilled vegetables please.
5 *I like* / *I'd like* some sushi, please.
6 How *is* / *was* your meal?
7 *Would you like* / *You like* a dessert?
8 *I'll have* / *I like* a coffee.
9 *We'll* / *We'd* like two coffees, please.
10 *Could* / *Would* I have the bill, please?

4 Which of these phrases in *italics* mean (a) '*Do you want ...?*', (b) '*I / We want ...*', or (c) neither.

1 *Do you like* sushi? ___
2 *Are you ready to* order? ___
3 *We like* sparkling water. ___
4 *We'd like* sparkling water. ___
5 *I have* sushi. ___
6 *I'll have* sushi. ___
7 *Would you like* a dessert? ___
8 *Could I have* the bill? ___

5 Work with a partner. Take turns to be a customer and a waiter at the café. Use the menu and practise ordering food.

6 Read these sentences and complete the rules with the words in bold.

Would you like ***some*** *french fries?*
We'd like ***a*** *bottle of sparkling water.*
I'd like ***some*** *sushi, please.*

1 Use ________ / *an* with singular, countable nouns.
2 Use ________ with plural countable nouns and uncountable nouns.

7 Work with a partner. Write *a* / *an* or *some* next to these words.

1 ___*a*___ (cup of) coffee

2 ___*some*___ coffee

3 ________ sushi

4 ________ salad

5 ________ cheese

6 ________ sandwich

7 ________ french fries

8 ________ steak

» For more exercises, go to **Practice file 6** on page 88.

8 Think of your last trip abroad. Was it for business or pleasure? How were the restaurants? Did you try some local dishes? What food did you eat? Tell the class.

ⓘ » Interactive Workbook » **Glossary**

Tip | countable and uncountable nouns

Some nouns are countable:
1 apple, 2 apples, 1 bottle, 3 bottles
Some nouns are uncountable:
sushi, chicken
Some nouns can be both:
I'd like ***a*** *(cup of) coffee.*
Can I have ***some*** *coffee?*

Language at work | Past simple: irregular verbs | Time expressions

1 **What are trade fairs? Who goes to them?**

2 **Read about this Industry Expo.**

1 What type of industry was it for?
2 When and where was it?
3 Where were manufacturers, suppliers, and other representatives from?
4 Does your business or industry have similar events?

Recent events

Textile Industry Expo Date: 1–4 August, 2009

Venue: Ho Chi Minh City International Exhibition & Convention Center, Vietnam

Almost 100 companies went to this year's Industry Expo. Manufacturers and suppliers from China, the Republic of Korea, India, Taiwan, and Hong Kong met Vietnamese producers, and two companies from Austria and Italy also had representatives at the event.

Don't miss this event next year. Click here for early registration.

3 **There are three verbs in the description of the Expo. Underline them. Do they describe the past or present?**

4 **34▷ Listen to Giang and Enzo meet at the Expo.**

1 Where is Enzo from?
2 What do they give each other?
3 How did they travel to the Expo?

5 **34▷ Listen again. Number these verbs in the order you hear them.**

came ___ took _1_ flew ___
had ___ were ___ left ___ met ___

6 **Write the verbs in 2 and 5 next to the infinitive.**

1 be – *was*
2 take – ________
3 go – ________
4 meet – ________
5 have – ________
6 leave – ________
7 come – ________
8 fly – ________

7 **Read this extract from Enzo and Giang's conversation. Complete the timeline with the time expressions in bold.**

I came to Ho Chi Minh City **last night**, but I left Bologna **two days ago**. I flew to Milan and then to Shanghai. I had a day in Shanghai, so I met some colleagues there **yesterday**.

a year ago — last month — ________ — ________ — ________ — this morning

8 **Work with a partner. Describe your last trip. Talk about some of the following and use time expressions.**

- where you went
- how long the journey took
- when you left / arrived
- when you came home
- what meeting (conference) you had
- where you left from
- who you met

9 35▷ **Listen to Giang ask Enzo about his career. Complete these questions.**

1 How did you ________ a sales manager in textiles?
2 Why did you ________?
3 When did you ________ your current company?

10 35▷ **Listen again. What are Enzo's answers?**

» For more information and exercises, go to **Practice file 6** on page 89.

11 **Work with a partner.**

1 Write five sentences about your career using time expressions.
Example: *I went to University in 1999.*
I studied …
2 Swap your sentences. Ask and answer questions about your careers. Begin with the question: *How did you become a …* (job title)?

Practically speaking | How to describe a trip

1 **Which adjectives below describe**

- a hotel?
- a meal or the food?
- a city or country?
- a journey?
- a presentation?

nice good boring delicious comfortable interesting
OK terrible fine

2 **Work with a partner. Look at some photographs from a trip. Take turns to ask and answer questions. Student A, turn to file 14 on page 106. Student B, turn to file 46 on page 114.**

3 **Now ask your partner about their most recent trip.**
Example: *How was the flight? How was the hotel?*

Business communication | Making conversation

1 How can you start a conversation in these two situations?

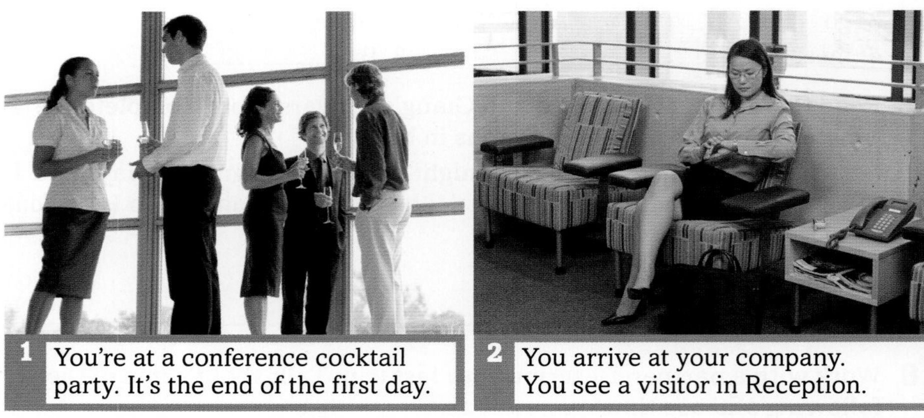

1 You're at a conference cocktail party. It's the end of the first day.

2 You arrive at your company. You see a visitor in Reception.

2 36,37▷ **Listen to two conversations and match them to situations 1 and 2 above.**

3 36▷ **Match phrases 1–8 to responses a–h, then listen again and check.**

1 Can I join you? ___
2 I hear you work for GST. ___
3 My name's Simon Turing. ___
4 What do you think of the conference? ___
5 Do you come here every year? ___
6 Do you know a lot of people here? ___
7 Would you like another drink? ___
8 Please excuse me. ___

a Very interesting.
b Sure. See you later maybe.
c Yes, of course.
d No, not many.
e Pleased to meet you.
f No, thanks. I'm fine.
g Yes, that's right.
h No, this is my first time.

4 Work with a partner. You are at a conference. Practise this conversation.

- start the conversation
- talk about the conference
- offer something
- end the conversation.

5 37▷ **Work with a partner. Think of possible responses to these sentences, then listen again and compare your answers.**

1 Can I help you?
2 Is this your first time here?
3 Please go in and take a seat.
4 Can I get you something?
5 Nice talking to you.

» For more exercises, go to **Practice file 6** on page 88.

6 Work with a partner. Practise this conversation.

- start a conversation with a visitor in Reception
- offer to take him / her to a colleague's office
- offer something to drink
- end the conversation

7 Work with a partner. Student A, turn to File 18 on page 107. Student B, turn to File 43 on page 113.

ⓘ » Interactive Workbook » **Email** and » **Exercises and Tests**

Key expressions

Starting a conversation
Can I join you?
I hear you work for ...
Is this your first time ...?
What do you think of ...?

Offering
Can I help you?
Can I get you something?
Would you like another ...?
Please take a seat. / Please go in and take a seat.

Responding
Yes, please.
Yes, of course.
Yes, that's right.
No, thanks. (I'm fine).

Finishing a conversation
Please excuse me.
Nice talking to you.
See you later.

ⓘ » Interactive Workbook » **Phrasebank**

The socializing game

Play the socializing game with a partner.

Choose a square.
On a blue square, read the question or sentence, and then respond. On a brown square, read the answer and ask an appropriate question.
If you are right, you win the square.
Then your partner chooses a square and does the same.
Try to complete a line of five squares across (➡), down (⬇), or diagonally (↘) before your partner.

Examples:

Do you like fish?	*You say:* *Yes, and I really like sushi.*
Do ...? No, not many.	*You say:* *Do you know many people here?*

Is this ...? No, I was here last year.	What would you like to drink?	**How ...?** Fine. There was no traffic on the roads.	When did you join your company?	**Can I ...?** Yes, please. I'll have a coffee.
My name's Rudolf.	**Can ...?** Yes, sure. Take a seat.	**I hear ...** Yes, it's a great company.	Nice talking to you.	When did you start your job?
What ...? It's very interesting.	**Would ...?** No, thanks. I'm fine.	Please excuse me.	Would you like a side dish with that?	**Could I ...?** Certainly. It's €25, please.
Are you ready to order?	**How ...?** Delicious! Thank you.	Where did you go on holiday last year?	**How ...?** My room was a bit small, but it was very comfortable.	When did you last travel by plane?
Would you like a dessert?	How did you become a ...(your job)?	**Do ...?** No, not every year, but I was here last year.	Would you like to order first?	**Can ...?** Yes, please. I have a lot of bags.

Activity

7 Departments

Learning objectives in this unit

- Describing responsibilities and departments
- Describing location and giving directions
- Showing a visitor round

Case study

- Designing the perfect workspace

Starting point

1 **How many departments does your company have? Can you name them?**

2 **Which department has a large number of employees? Which is a small department?**

3 **What does your department do?**

Working with words | Responsibilities and departments

1 **Read this article. Write these job titles in the career profiles.**

- Commercial Manager
- Customer Development Director
- Logistics Manager
- Financial Director

CAREER PROFILES

Find out about a career with Unilever. Read about some of the people who work for us around the world.

Tomas Jans

1 *Customer Development Director*, Argentina
He **manages** sales teams in Argentina and **plans** strategy. Teamwork is very important in his job. That's why he loves sport so much!

Guilherme Loureiro

2 ________________, Brazil
He's **in charge of** financial results and tax planning for the Unilever Group in Brazil. Because he's in Finance, he works with many different departments and **checks** their accounts.

Bala Malladi

3 ________________, India
Currently, he's **responsible for** new business ideas. For example, one new business project is to **develop** e-business in India.

Nevin Sindal

4 ________________, Turkey
She **deals with** delivery between factories, warehouses, and suppliers. In logistics, you **control** the movement of goods, so everything has to be on time.

2 **There are two verbs in bold in each profile. Match them to these definitions.**

Profile 1

a is the boss of people or a company: *manages*
b organizes (a project) in advance: *plans*

Profile 2

a makes sure information is correct: ________
b manages someone or something: ________

Profile 3

a become bigger and more successful: ________
b is the person in charge of something: ________

Profile 4

a does the tasks of a job: ________
b make something do what you want: ________

3 <u>Underline</u> **the correct verb in *italics*.**

1 I'm a customer services assistant. I *deal with* / *'m in charge of* customers every day.
2 Jessica *plans* / *is responsible for* ten people in her section.
3 The IT department *develops* / *controls* the computers in all the offices.
4 Production deals with the products, but R&D *manages* / *develops* new products.
5 I work for Guilherme, the Financial Director. Sometimes he asks me to *control* / *check* his work for him. He doesn't want to make any mistakes!

4 **Work with a partner. Make sentences about these jobs using the verbs in 2.**

Example: *An air traffic controller controls the movement of aeroplanes.*

air traffic controller / movement of aeroplanes

teachers / students

engineer / projects

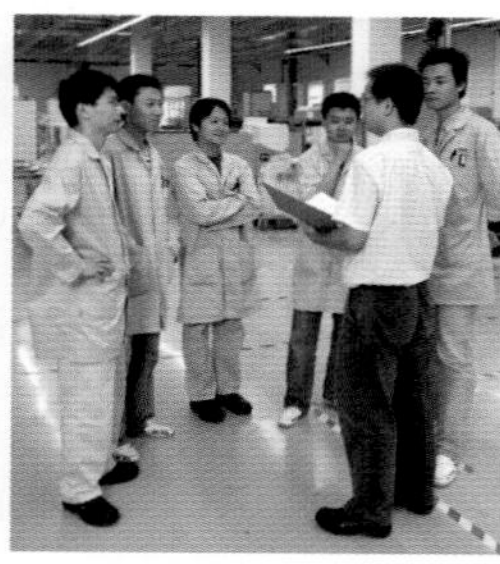
team leaders / team

production manager / factory

5 **Work with the same partner. Make sentences about these departments using words in the table.**

Example: *Logistics plans deliveries from suppliers.*

Logistics Finance Sales Information Technology (IT) Research and Development (R&D) Human Resources (HR) Marketing Customer Services Production	works with is responsible for deals with plans controls is in charge of manages develops checks organizes	suppliers customers information employees deliveries machinery other departments products money computers

» For more exercises, go to **Practice file 7** on page 90.

6 **38▷ We can pronounce words ending in *-s* with /s/, /z/, or /ɪz/. Listen and write the sounds.**

Example: *works* /s/ *is* /z/ *manages* /ɪz/

1 deals ___	4 products ___	7 controls ___
2 plans ___	5 departments ___	8 develops ___
3 organizes ___	6 computers ___	9 resources ___

7 **Write a short job profile for you, then read it to your partner.**

8 **Take turns to describe some departments in your company. Try to guess the department your partner describes.**

Example: ***A*** *This department works with customers.*
B *Sales.*
A *Correct.*

ⓘ » Interactive Workbook » **Glossary**

Tip | Word building

When you learn a new word, you can make more words with it:
manage – manager
produce – products, production
purchase – purchasing
deliver – delivery

Language at work | Prepositions of place and movement

1 Jim Berman plans a visit to Olivia Gonzalez's company. Read Olivia's email to Jim. There is one mistake in her directions. Look at the map and find the mistake.

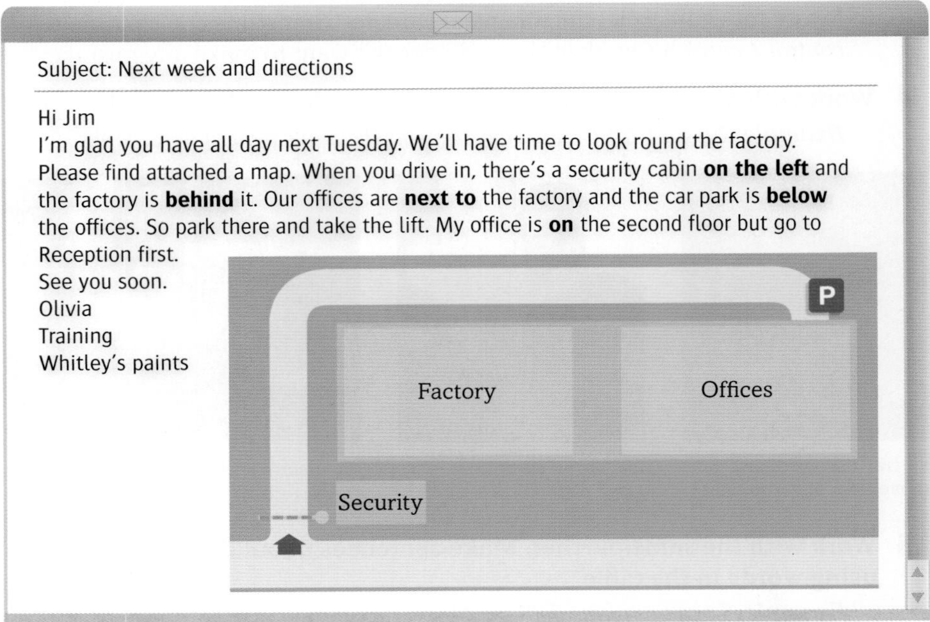

Subject: Next week and directions

Hi Jim

I'm glad you have all day next Tuesday. We'll have time to look round the factory. Please find attached a map. When you drive in, there's a security cabin **on the left** and the factory is **behind** it. Our offices are **next to** the factory and the car park is **below** the offices. So park there and take the lift. My office is **on** the second floor but go to Reception first.

See you soon.

Olivia

Training

Whitley's paints

2 Look at this office plan. Underline the correct words in *italics*.

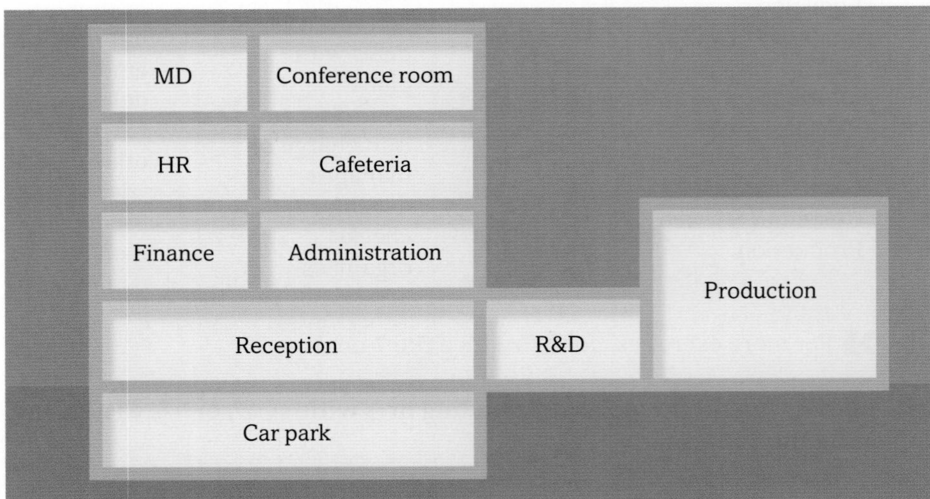

1 Production is on the *left* / *right* of Reception.
2 Finance is *above* / *below* HR.
3 The MD's office is *between* / *next to* the conference room.
4 The cafeteria is on the *second* / *third* floor.
5 The car park is *in front of* / *below* Reception.
6 R&D is *in* / *between* Reception and Production.

3 Work with a partner. Student A, turn to File 15 on page 106. Student B, turn to File 47 on page 114.

4 Work with a partner. Describe where rooms and departments are in your company. Where is your office?

Tip | UK and US English

British and American English have some vocabulary differences:

UK English	US English
ground floor	*first floor*
toilet	*restroom*
lift	*elevator*

5 39▷ **Jim arrives at the security cabin. Listen and complete the security man's directions.**

You go [1]________ this road and turn right. Go [2]________ the factory to the offices, but don't park there. Look for the car park sign and drive [3]________ below the offices and go [4]________ the car park there.

6 Match the prepositions of movement in 5 to these diagrams.

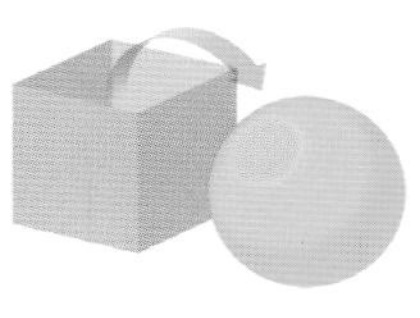

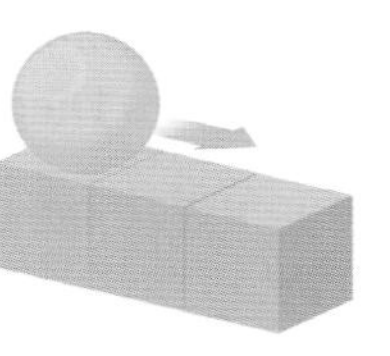
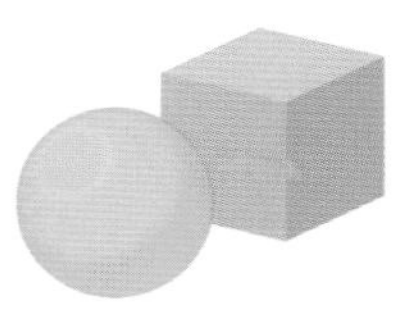

1 *out of* 2 *up* 3 ________ 4 ________ 5 ________ 6 ________

» For more information and exercises, go to **Practice file 7** on page 91.

7 Work with a partner. Take turns to give directions from where you are now to these places. Guess which place your partner gives directions to.

Example: *Go past the lift and turn left ...*

Reception *the cafeteria* *the lifts or stairs* *your favourite cafe*
the bank *your car* *the train station* *a cinema*

Practically speaking | How to use *this, that, these,* and *those*

1 Complete this conversation with *this, that, these,* or *those*.

1 ________ is your visitor's pass.

2 ________ are two of my colleagues.

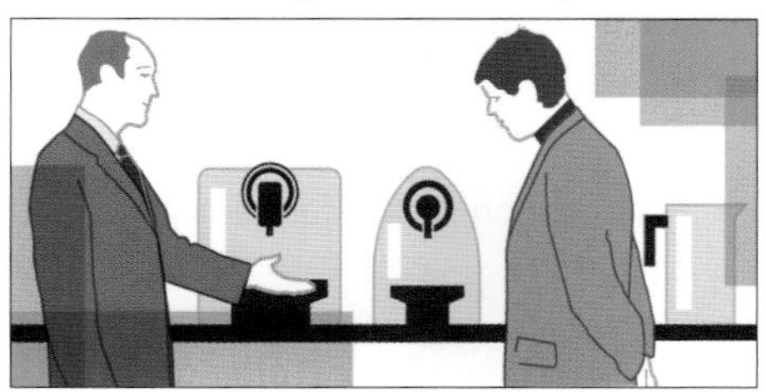

3 ________ are our products.

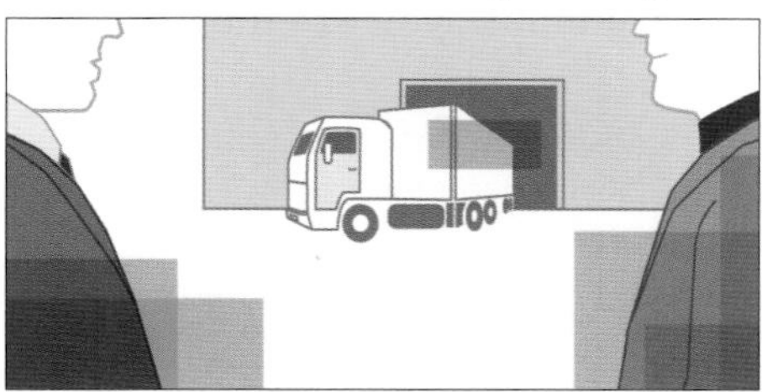

4 What is ________ building?
It's the warehouse.

2 Work with a partner. Practise the conversation in 1.

3 Work with a partner. Take turns to show each other objects and people in the room.

Example: *This is my desk.*
Is that your book?
Those are friends of mine.

Tip | Giving directions and instructions

Use the imperative form of the verb to give directions and instructions:

Go *along this road.*
Enter *your password.*

Sometimes we use *You* + verb to be more polite:

You go *along this road and turn left.*

Business communication | Showing a visitor round

1 **When a visitor arrives at your company, where do they go first? Through a security gate? To Reception? Do they sign in?**

2 **40▷ Jim Berman arrives at Reception. Listen to three parts of his visit and answer 1–3.**

1 What does the receptionist give him?
2 Does Jim want a coffee?
3 What does Diego deal with?

3 **Complete these phrases with verbs from the list.**

sign see is show like take introduce have will find

1 I ________ an appointment with Olivia Gonzalez. _V_
2 Can you ________ here, please? __
3 This ________ your visitor's pass. __
4 Please ________ a seat. __
5 Ms Gonzalez ________ be right down. __
6 Nice to ________ you again. __
7 Did you ________ us OK? __
8 Would you ________ a coffee? __
9 Let me ________ you round. __
10 Let me ________ you to Diego. __

4 **Now write who says each expression, the receptionist (*R*), the visitor (*V*), or the host (*H*).**

5 **40▷ Listen again.**

1 Check your answers in **3** and **4**.
2 What question does Jim ask about Production?
3 Think of three more questions a visitor could ask about a place of work.

» For more exercises, go to **Practice File 7** on page 90.

6 **Work with a partner. Practise a similar conversation. Follow the flowchart below. Student A, it is your company. You are the receptionist and the host. Student B, you are the visitor. Arrive at Reception and ask to see your host.**

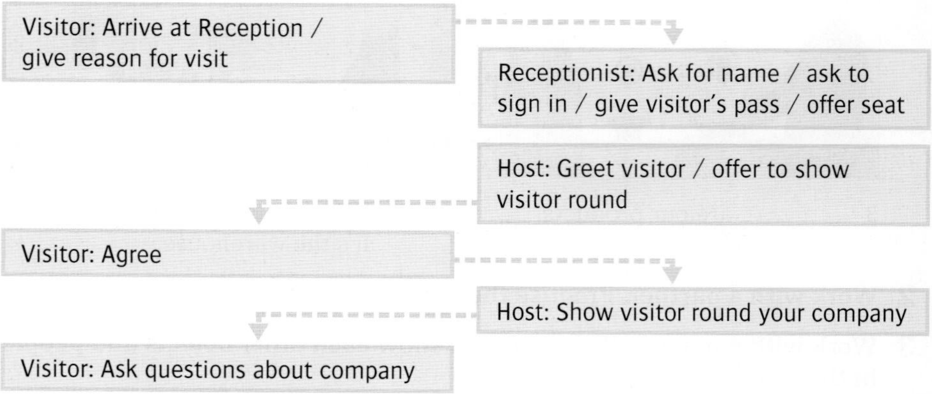

Visitor: Arrive at Reception / give reason for visit

Receptionist: Ask for name / ask to sign in / give visitor's pass / offer seat

Host: Greet visitor / offer to show visitor round

Visitor: Agree

Host: Show visitor round your company

Visitor: Ask questions about company

ⓘ » Interactive Workbook » **Email** and » **Exercises and Tests**

Key expressions

Arriving at Reception / Security
Good morning. I have an appointment with ...
Can you sign here, please?
This is your visitor's pass.
Take a seat. [Ms Gonzalez] will be right down.

Meeting your visitor / host
Nice to meet / see you (again).
Did you find us OK?
Would you like a coffee?

Showing your visitor round
Let me show you round.
This is ..., and that's ...
Let me introduce you to ...
He's in charge of ...

ⓘ » Interactive Workbook
» **Phrasebank**

Designing the perfect workspace

Background

New offices for PFIZER

In 2005, the Czech branch of the pharmaceuticals company, Pfizer, moved into its new offices. The original offices didn't have many meeting spaces, so it was difficult for teams and departments to work well together. The new offices are a better place for teams and communication. Inside, there are a lot of open spaces for employees to meet and talk: coffee areas, meeting rooms, etc. The staff cafeteria seats 100 people and has a garden which can be used for meetings too. The offices, though, are small, so people can concentrate when they need to. Communication between the departments was also very important. So the Medical, Marketing, and Sales Departments are connected by stairs and small meeting areas between the floors. Altogether, the new offices are a comfortable place to work, with a balance of open spaces for good communication, and small spaces for individual work.

Discussion

1 **How are Pfizer's new offices different from the old ones?**

2 **Do the staff work in big or small offices?**

3 **How does the design help departments to work together?**

4 **What is your workspace like? Do you have a lot of open spaces? Are the different departments well located?**

Task

1 **Work in small groups. Talk about your company. Who is responsible for what? Who works with who? Who needs to communicate with who? How is your office / department designed?**

2 **Design your perfect office or workspace so everyone can do their job well and communicate easily with their colleagues.**

3 **Present your new workspace to the rest of the class.**

Case study

8 Employment

Learning objectives in this unit

- Talking about professional qualities, skills, and experience
- Saying what you are doing and talking about trends
- Telling the time
- Arranging to meet

Activity

- The right person for the job

Starting point

1 How many employees are there in your company / your department / your office?

2 How does your company recruit new employees? Does it have a Human Resources Department?

Working with words | Employment

1 Read these job adverts.

1 What type of company is it?
2 Find two words that mean the same as *job*.
3 Which job needs a particular skill? What is it?

We are currently offering three positions for the right people:

Summer placement

Are you an **energetic** student with ambition? Get some work experience this summer. Every June–August we employ a **friendly** young person to help in our offices. Learn new skills and earn some money.

Web editor

We are looking for an **imaginative** but **focused** web editor to join our team. You are a **practical** person who can deal with problems on your own.

Website production assistant

This post needs a **careful** and **patient** person with basic skills in HTML. You assist **experienced** web producers and receive training.

Click here for more details

2 Match the adjectives in bold in 1 to definitions 1–8.

1 thinks about things and does not make mistakes ________
2 can deal with everyday problems ________
3 has new and exciting ideas ________
4 very active and lots of energy ________
5 can work on one job for a long time ________
6 kind and helpful ________
7 has lots of skills and knowledge in the job ________
8 can wait for a long time ________

3 41▷ **Listen to these words. Write the number of syllables and underline the stress.**

energetic *4*	imaginative ___	careful ___	friendly ___
practical ___	focused ___	patient ___	experienced ___

Now listen again and repeat the words.

4 **Work with a partner. Take turns to choose adjectives from 2 to describe these jobs. You can use more than one adjective. Guess what job your partner describes.**

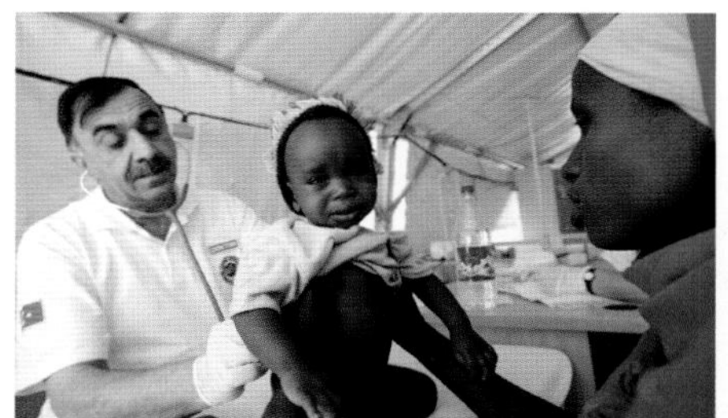

5 42▷ **Listen to Anton and Sandra in the HR Department of the company in 1. They are discussing candidates for the jobs. Make notes about Monica and Roberto in the table.**

	Monica	Roberto
Personal qualities	*friendly*	
Current situation		
Skills and experience		
Qualifications		

6 42▷ **Listen again and match 1–5 to a–e.**

1 She has a lot ___
2 She's good ___
3 He has a ___
4 He doesn't have ___
5 He isn't very ___

a … good at working on his own.
b … of experience in book editing.
c … any experience in editing.
d … qualification in IT.
e … at editing websites.

» For more exercises, go to **Practice file 8** on page 92.

7 **Work with a partner. Tell your partner about your job.**

1 What qualities do you need to do your job?
2 What skills, experience, and qualifications do you have?

8 **Work with another pair and present your partner to them.**

ⓘ » Interactive Workbook » **Glossary**

Tip | *experience in + -ing*

Use the *-ing* form after *experience in:*

She has a lot of experience in book editing.
He doesn't have any experience in editing.

Language at work | Present continuous

1 43▷ **Listen to three conversations in an office. Why are the people busy at the moment?**

2 44▷ **Listen to the first conversation again. Complete the conversation using the words in brackets.**

A Come on Sandra. It's 12 o'clock. Let's go for lunch.
B Sorry, I [1] *'m not going* __________ (not / go) for lunch today. There's no time.
A Why? What [2] __________ (you / do)?
B Anton and I [3] __________ (interview) someone.
A What? Now?
B It's for the web editor position. She [4] __________ (wait) in Reception. Sorry. See you later.
A Bye.

3 **The verbs in 2 are in the present continuous tense. What does this tense describe?**

- a general fact?
- a repeated action?
- an action or event now or around the moment of speaking?

4 **Complete these rules.**

1 the present continuous uses ________ + verb + *-ing*.
2 negative sentences use the negative form of the verb ________ .
3 questions use ________ + subject + ________ + *-ing*.

5 **Complete the next two conversations using the present continuous form of the verbs in brackets.**

A Where's Chantelle?
B She [1] __________ (not / work) here today. She's at home.
A Why?
B She [2] __________ (finish) her report. Her boss wants it for 7.30 tomorrow morning.

C Where [3] __________ (Bill and Sofia / go)?
D They [4] __________ (do) the training course for that new finance software all day.
C When are they back?
D At about a quarter to six.

6 45▷ **Listen to the two conversations again and check your answers to 5.**

7 **Match questions 1–5 to answers a–e.**

1 What are you doing at the moment? ___
2 Are you working on any interesting projects? ___
3 How are your English lessons? ___
4 Could you give me a hand? ___
5 What is the weather like today? ___

a It's raining.
b Sorry. I'm trying to finish these plans.
c I'm working with our partners in Italy.
d Yes, we are working on a new hospital in Cairo.
e They're difficult, but I'm making progress.

8 Work with a partner. Ask and answer questions 1–5 in **7**, giving answers for yourself.

9 Read this article.

1 <u>Underline</u> all the examples of the present continuous.
2 Do the verbs describe a *repeated action* or a *changing situation*?

Employment news: What is changing our working world?

Computers changed employment in the twentieth century, so what is changing our work and lives in this century?

- Employees aren't staying in the same job. Nowadays, the average employee starts a new job every three years.
- The number of women in work is rising and more women are working in higher positions.
- More people are working from home and deciding their own working hours.

10 Do you agree with the article? Is it true for you and your company? Tell the class.

» For more information and exercises, go to **Practice file 8** on page 93.

11 Make a list of current changes where you work. For example

- employ more staff
- spend more on training
- invest in research

12 Work with a partner. Tell your partner about the changes, using the present continuous. Try to give reasons for the changes.

Example: *We're employing more staff at the moment because we're receiving more orders.*

Practically speaking | How to tell the time

1 46▷ Listen to four conversations. Match the conversations to the times below.

A ___

B ___

C ___

D ___

2 Work with a partner. Ask and answer these questions.

1 What time did you start work today?
2 What time do you normally have lunch?
3 What time is it now?

3 Ask your partner three more *What time …?* questions.

Tip | *at / on*

Use the prepositions *at* and *on* with times and days of the week:

*I start work **at** eight o'clock.*
*Can we meet **on** Tuesday **at** three?*

Business communication | Arranging to meet

1 **When are you free this week? When are you busy?**

2 **47▷ A company has a plan for more staff to work from home. Kasia wants to arrange a meeting with the heads of department, Bruno, Dolores, and Chen. She calls Bruno first. Listen to the conversation. Put a cross (✗) when Kasia and Bruno are busy.**

Thursday	Kasia	Bruno
0800-0900		
0900-1000		
1000-1100		
1100-1200		
1200-1300		
1300-1400		
1400-1500		

3 **47▷ Listen again and complete these sentences.**

1 We need to ________ ________ the plan … .
2 ________ we ________ a meeting on Thursday …?
3 ________ two o'clock OK for you?
4 Sorry, I'm busy ________ .
5 ________ ________ the morning?
6 What time are you ________?
7 Nine thirty is ________ ________ me.
8 I ________ ________ between eight and ten.
9 ________ you ________ after that?
10 ________ ten fifteen good for you?
11 Yes, a quarter past ten on Thursday is ________ … .

4 **Put 1–11 from 3 into these categories.**

a Asking to meet: __, __
b Asking about times: __, __, __, __, __
c Saying when you are free: __, __
d Saying when you are busy: __, __

» For more exercises, go to **Practice file 8** on page 92.

5 **Work with a partner and arrange the meeting with Dolores. Student A, you are Kasia. Telephone Dolores about the meeting on Thursday. Student B, you are Dolores. Turn to File 44 on page 113.**

6 **Now arrange the meeting with Chen. Student A, you are Chen. Turn to File 17 on page 107. Student B, you are Bruno. Telephone Chen about the meeting.**

7 **Work in small groups. Arrange times this week for you all to**

- have a three-hour meeting
- have an extra English lesson
- interview people for the new receptionist position (two half days).

ⓘ » Interactive Workbook » **Email** and » **Exercises and Tests**

Key expressions

Asking to meet
Can we arrange a meeting?
We need to meet about …
I'd like to meet …

Asking about times
Is … OK?
Is … good for you?
What time are you free?
Are you free on / at …?
Can we meet on / at …?
Are you busy …?

Saying when you are free
… is good / fine for me.
I'm free on / at …

Saying you aren't free
Sorry, I'm busy then.
I can't meet …

ⓘ » Interactive Workbook
» **Phrasebank**

The right person for the job

Work with a partner. Your company is advertising two new jobs. You need to find the right person for the jobs. Follow stages 1 to 5 to find the right candidate.

STAGE 1 – The job advert

Complete these notes to describe the type of person you are looking for in each job.

Marketing assistant
Experience:
Qualities:

Administrative assistant
Experience:
Qualities:

STAGE 2 – Arranging the interviews

The job advert is written. You now need to arrange a day for interviews. Find a day when you are both free to interview people.

Student A, go to File 20 on page 108.
Student B, go to File 45 on page 113.

STAGE 3 – Preparing for the interview

With your partner, create two short candidate profiles for each job, for example, experience and knowledge needed for the job.
Decide on some questions you want to ask.

STAGE 4 – Holding the interviews

Join with another pair. Take turns to interview each person in the other pair for the job.

STAGE 5 – Choosing the candidate

Go back to your first partner.
Discuss each candidate and decide which one to choose for the job.

Activity

9 | Competition

Learning objectives in this unit

- Talking about competition
- Comparing products and companies
- Saying prices
- Comparing and choosing

Case study

- Making a supermarket competitive

Starting point

1 Do you work in a competitive industry / business?

2 Who are your competitors, locally and globally?

3 Where are they?

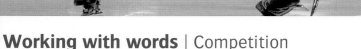

Working with words | Competition

1 48▷ **Listen to a manager talking about the company Accor, and complete this fact file.**

1 ___________ employees

2 In nearly ___________ countries

3 Over ___________ hotels worldwide

MARKET SEGMENTS AND LOCATION

PRICE	HOTEL CHAIN	WHERE
Budget	Motel 6	4___________
Economy	5___________	Asia-Pacific
Mid-range	6___________	worldwide
Top range	Sofitel	worldwide

Sofitel Magic Lagoon Khao Lak Hotel, Phuket, Thailand

2 **Discuss these questions in small groups.**

1 Which of these do you think are important for hotels to be competitive?

2 When you choose a hotel, which three are most important?

Price ___	Delivery time ___
Choice and range ___	Staff ___
Technology ___	Quality ___
Services ___	Something else ___
Location ___	

3 48▷ **Listen to the manager again and tick (✓) the areas she mentions.**

4 **Work with a partner. Discuss which categories in 2 are important for you and your competitors. Do you offer something special?**

5 49▷ **Complete these sentences with adjectives from the list. Then listen and check your answers.**

low expensive wide up-to-date good high cheap friendly

1 We can offer all our customers a ________ choice.

2 They are ________-price hotels and offer the customer a ________ option.

3 They offer very ________ service with ________ staff.

4 The quality at a Novotel hotel is very ________ with modern, ________ business facilities.

5 A Sofitel hotel is ________, but it offers five-star quality.

6 **Work with a partner. Use the adjectives in A to describe the items in B. You can use some adjectives more than once.**

Example: *low / high prices*
low / high quality

A	B
low / high good / bad cheap / expensive fast / slow up-to-date wide	prices choice and range location technology quality service delivery time

» For more exercises, go to **Practice file 9** on page 94.

7 **Prepare a short presentation on how your company (or a company you know well) is competitive.**

- Explain how you are competitive in your industry (e.g. price, choice)
- Explain what your company offers with adjectives from **6**.
  Example: *We offer good service.*

8 **Give your presentation to your partner or to the class.**

ⓘ » Interactive Workbook » **Glossary**

Language at work | Comparatives

1 **Do you normally buy these products or services from a shop / office or from a website? Why? Compare your answers with the rest of the class.**

- music
- holidays or airline tickets
- clothes
- property
- food and drink
- financial advice and loans
- electrical goods

2 **Where does your company sell its products or services? In shops, over the Internet, or elsewhere?**

3 50▷ **Listen to these interviews with two business owners. Who runs**

- a web-based mail order company?
- a high street shop?

4 50▷ **They describe the competitive advantages of their companies. Listen again and complete this table.**

Company 1	Company 2
a [1]________ service	[5]________ prices
staff are [2]________ ________	[6]________ stocks
staff are [3]________	[7]________ delivery
products are [4]________ ________	a [8]________ choice

5 **Complete these rules for forming comparatives.**

1. One-syllable adjectives (*low*, *fast*, etc.): add ___.
2. Adjectives ending in *-y* (*friendly*, etc.): replace the *-y* with ___.
3. Long adjectives (*experienced*, *up-to-date*, etc.): put ________ before the adjective.
4. Some adjectives are irregular: *good* → ________, *bad* → *worse*.

6 **Complete this text with the comparative forms of the adjectives in brackets.**

Multichannel Selling

Modern companies use multichannel selling. In the past, customers went to a high street shop because staff were [1]*friendlier* (friendly) and gave [2]________ (good) advice. But they also preferred online shopping because it offered a [3]________ (wide) selection with [4]________ (cheap) prices. Nowadays, successful companies must offer customers both [5]________ (easy) shopping with a website, and [6]________ (experienced) help from a high street shop.

» For more information and exercises, go to **Practice File 9** on page 95.

7 **Work with a partner. Make sentences from the table below. Student A begins the sentence. Student B finishes the sentence. Change roles after each sentence.**

Example: ***A*** *Supermarkets have a wider choice …*
B *Supermarkets have a wider choice than small shops.*

A			B
DVDs Supermarkets English Wine Sales managers Flying	wide choice difficult / easy to learn up-to-date big expensive / cheap fast low prices experienced	than …	small shops mineral water sea travel CDs Chinese sales reps

8 **Work with a partner. Take turns to compare your company with a competitor. Compare areas such as**

- price
- products / service
- choice
- staff
- delivery.

Example: *My company is more expensive than our competitor, but we offer a higher quality service.*

Practically speaking | How to say prices

1 51▷ **Listen and tick (✓) the prices you hear.**

¥2,860 ___	$50 ___	€29.99 ___	¥170 ___	€11.75 ___
$26.80 ___	$28.60 ___	¥2,690 ___	¥2,960 ___	$7.15 ___
$500 ___	€17.50 ___	$7.50 ___	€11.79 ___	$30 ___

2 51▷ **Listen again and complete this price information.**

1 Price of phone: ________
Price of calls per month: ________ for ten hours
________ for five hours

2 Delivery free on orders of ________ or more
Delivery per item: ________
Delivery for four items: ________

3 Normal price: ________
Discount with customer card: ________
Final price: ________

3 **Work with a partner. Take turns saying the prices you ticked in 1.**

Business communication | Comparing and choosing

Javier Sampedro works for a chain of shops. His company wants to update its website and sell products online. Javier asked two web design companies, Weblines and ITE, for quotes. He compares the quotes for his managing director at their weekly meeting.

1 52▷ **Listen and complete the table.**

	Weblines	ITE
Lower prices?		✓
Smaller company?		
Older company?		
Better quality of work?		
More experience with online businesses?		
Faster delivery?		

2 52▷ **Listen again and complete these sentences.**

a How do they ________?
b ITE is ________.
c Are they ________?
d The quality is ________.
e The ________ of ITE is the two people have experience in the online marketing and sales industry.
f The ________ of Weblines is they don't usually work with online businesses.
g There's no ________.
h I ________ ITE.
i Let's ________ them.

3 Put a–i in 2 into categories 1–4.

1 Asking about differences: *a* , ___
2 Talking about similarities: ___ , ___
3 Talking about differences: ___ , ___ , ___
4 Choosing: ___ , ___

4 Work with a partner. Student A, ask Student B about differences and choose one from each pair.

- Transportation for work: a motorbike or a bicycle?
- Employ a new person for your department: put an advert in a newspaper or use a recruitment agency?
- English lessons: in a classroom with a teacher or online?

Student B, talk about the similarities and differences.

Example: **A** *I want a motorbike or a bicycle for work. How do they compare?*
B *A bicycle is cheaper, but …*

Now change roles and discuss these.

- Food for a conference: local or foreign dishes?
- A two-day training course: at work during the week or in a five-star hotel at the weekend?
- A holiday this summer: at home or abroad?

» For more exercises, go to **Practice file 9** on page 94.

5 Work with a partner and discuss some quotes. Student A, turn to file 19 on page 107. Student B, turn to file 48 on page 115.

ⓘ » Interactive Workbook » **Email** and » **Exercises and Tests**

Key expressions

Asking about differences
What's the difference?
How do they compare?
Are they better?

Talking about similarities
X does ..., but Y also ...
There's no difference.
… is similar (to …)

Talking about differences
They're (cheap)er / more ...
The advantage of ... is ...
The disadvantage is ...

Choosing
Let's choose ...
This one's better.
I prefer ...

ⓘ » Interactive Workbook
» **Phrasebank**

Making a supermarket competitive

Background

Shopping around

Competition between supermarkets is very strong. In the UK there are four major supermarkets and Morrisons is number four. The image of Morrisons is low prices, a wide range of food, and friendly staff.

Tesco, the number one supermarket, has small shops in towns and big shops outside towns. It also has a healthy eating range of food and a loyalty card for regular customers. Tesco sells non-food products too like TVs, washing machines, and furniture.

Sainsbury's has an expensive image, but it has some economy products, and with the help of English chef, Jamie Oliver, more people shop there now. It has many 'green' and fair-trade products too, and quality is very important. Sainsbury's trains all its staff to know more about its products.

Discussion

1 **What do the three supermarkets do to stay competitive?**

2 **Which supermarket do you shop at? Why do you go there?**

3 **Which points in the text are important for you when you shop at a supermarket?**

Task

1 **You work for Morrisons. You need to find ways to improve its competitiveness. Work in groups of four, and divide into Pair A and Pair B. Read your information below.**

Pair A

You work in the team for product selection. What changes can you make so Morrisons is more competitive? Make a list of five ideas. Think about

- Product range
- Product price
- Where do your products come from?
- Why do / don't *you* buy certain products?

Pair B

You work in the team for company image. What changes can you make so Morrisons is more competitive? Make a list of five ideas. Think about

- Staff training
- Staff experience
- Company image
- What image is good for a supermarket?

2 **Now hold a meeting and present your ideas to the other pair. Decide on five ideas you want to keep.**

3 **Turn to File 21 on page 108 to read what Morrisons did. How do your ideas compare?**

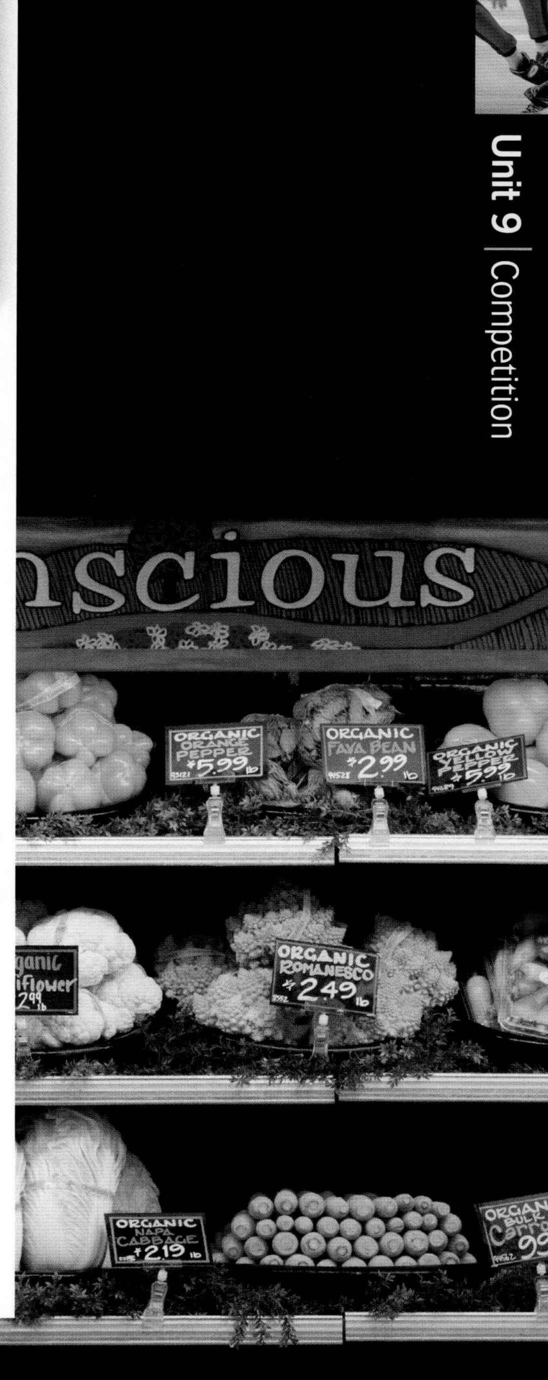

10 Teamwork

Learning objectives in this unit

- Talking about teams
- Discussing problems
- Talking about present and future arrangements
- Choosing the best options
- Responding to news
- Giving opinions

Case study

- Changing the way you work

Starting point

1. Do you usually work alone or in a team?
2. What are the advantages of working in a team?
3. When you make decisions, do you always ask for other opinions?
4. Do you have your best ideas on your own or with others?

Working with words | Working in teams

1 **Read about the Gore company. Which of their working methods are similar in your company?**

'Who's my boss?'

W.L. Gore & Associates is well known for its GORE-TEX® fabrics. Wilbert and Genevieve Gore started the company in 1958. It has no bosses or job titles. The company's rules for business are:

1 SMALL TEAMS
Everyone knows each other and makes decisions together.

2 NO BOSSES
You work in a team, but there are no job titles and no bosses.

3 THE LONG VIEW
It often takes years to solve problems and find solutions for new products.

4 TIME TO TALK
You attend meetings. Face-to-face communication is better than memos and emails.

5 EVERYONE'S A LEADER
You develop ideas to share with your team, and you plan new projects.

2 Tick (✓) the phrases you think people say at Gore.

1 I don't like working with other people. ___
2 I don't know – ask the boss. ___
3 Let's have a meeting. ___
4 It took a long time, but we have a great product. ___
5 It's not my job to think of new ideas. ___
6 I need to speak to the team before I make a decision. ___

3 Match 1–6 to a–f, then check your answers in the text in 1.

1 attend ___	a decisions
2 make ___	b problems
3 work ___	c solutions
4 develop ___	d meetings
5 find ___	e in a team
6 solve ___	f ideas

4 Complete these questions.

1 What ________ do you make?
2 What meetings did you ________ last month?
3 Do you ________ in a team, or alone?
4 What do you do when you want to ________ a problem?
5 What is a good time of day to ________ new ideas?
6 How do you feel when you find a ________ to a problem?

5 Work with a partner. Ask and answer the questions in 4.

6 53▷ **Listen to three conversations. In each conversation what is the problem?**

7 53▷ **Listen again and complete 1–6 with an adjective.**

1 There's a ________ problem with ...
2 Yes, that's a ________ idea!
3 I have a really ________ problem.
4 That's a ________ decision.
5 What's your ________ decision?
6 No. That's a ________ idea.

» For more exercises, go to **Practice file 10** on page 96.

8 Work with a partner. Discuss these problems using the expressions in 3 and 7.

- An important customer wants a 20% discount on all orders. You normally offer 10%.
- Someone in your team is off sick for two weeks. You need to finish your project this Friday.
- You have to take a new client for dinner. You need to decide where to go.
- Two people in your team are good at their jobs, but there is a personality problem: they cannot work together and always disagree in meetings.

9 Think of a problem you have at work. Tell your partner and discuss it. Can you solve the problem?

» Interactive Workbook » **Glossary**

Tip | collocations

Some words sound natural together. For example:
make decisions, solve problems
We call them collocations.

Language at work | Present continuous | Superlatives

1 What type of problems are these, technical, personnel, or supply?

1 A member of staff spends too much time surfing the Internet.
2 The warehouse is nearly empty.
3 You can't open your email attachments.

RICHARD, Production Manager, Rio

ADRIANA, Technical Manager, Rio

PEDRO, Line Manager, Recife Factory

2 54▷ Listen to this meeting between Richard and Adriana. Which problems do they discuss below?

An employee is often late.
The new components for the production line don't work.
There are technical problems in the factories.
There is a delay with flights to Recife.

3 Complete these questions using the present continuous of the verbs in brackets.

1 Who ________ Jorge ________ to *at the moment*? (speak)
2 ________ Production Line 1 *still* ________ problems? (have)
3 ________ the components ________ *later today*? (arrive)
4 *When* ________ Adriana ________ to Recife? (go)
5 ________ Marcio ________ with the new components *when Adriana is in Recife*? (deal)
6 Who ________ Adriana ________ in Recife *tomorrow*? (meet)

4 54▷ Listen to the meeting again, and answer the questions in 3.

5 Which questions in 3 talk about

- the present?
- the future?

Use the words in *italics* in 3 to help you.

6 Work with a partner. Take turns to ask and answer questions using ideas in the table.

***Example**: Are you studying English at the moment?*

Is / Are What is / are When is / are	you your colleagues your team your department	study leave start go speak arrive meet	at the moment? later today? tomorrow? when ...?

7 55▷Adriana is visiting the factory in Recife. She telephones Richard. Listen to the conversation. Are these sentences true (*T*) or false (*F*)?

1 The problem at the factory is *small*. ___
2 The new components were *the most expensive*. ___
3 The new components were *the best* idea. ___
4 Pedro thinks the *new* components are *better* than the old. ___
5 Personnel problems at the factory are *bigger* than technical problems. ___
6 Staff turnover in Recife is *the highest*. ___
7 The team is *the biggest* problem. ___

8 Which sentences in 7

a don't compare anything? ___
b compare two things (with the comparative form)? ___, ___
c compare one thing with all other things? ___, ___, ___, ___

9 **The sentences in 8c use the superlative form. Complete these rules for forming superlatives.**

1 One-syllable adjectives (*small*, etc.): add ___.
2 Long adjectives (*expensive*, *up-to-date*, etc.): put ________ before the adjective.
3 Some adjectives are irregular: *good* → ________, *bad* → *worst*.

10 **Three days later, Richard sends this email. Complete it with the superlative form of the words in brackets.**

Hi Adriana,

How was your trip? We have a lot of things to discuss, but [1]________________ (important) decision at the moment is what to do with Pedro:

fire him? offer him a different job in Recife? move him to Rio?

What's [2]________________ (good) solution? Perhaps [3]________________ (cheap) solution is to offer Pedro a new job in Recife. What do you think?

Richard

» For more information and exercises, go to **Practice file 10** on page 97.

11 **Work with a partner. You need to find a new line manager for Recife. Turn to File 22 on page 108.**

12 **Think of two or three answers for the following. Then tell your partner and compare them. Use the superlatives in brackets.**

Example: *I'm having a few problems at work ... but the biggest problem I have is ...*

- current problems you are having at work (smallest? biggest?)
- new products in your home or at work (newest? most expensive?)
- new ideas you had this week (worst? best?)

Practically speaking | How to respond to news

1 **Put these expressions for responding to news into categories 1–3.**

a Oh no. That's terrible.
b Really? How amazing.
c Great. That's fantastic!
d Wow. That is surprising.
e I'm sorry. How disappointing.
f Good. That's excellent news.

1 Responding to good news: ___, ___
2 Responding to bad news: ___, ___
3 Showing surprise: ___, ___

2 **56▷ Listen and underline the stressed words and syllables in the expressions in 1, then listen again and repeat the expressions.**

3 **Work with a partner. Student A, turn to File 23 on page 108. Student B, turn to File 49 on page 115. Respond to each other's news.**

4 **Think of more news from your job or home. Tell your partner and respond to his / her news.**

Business communication | Giving opinions

1 **Papotech, an office supply company, is currently having two problems:**

- **staff are leaving**
- **customers are complaining**

The Director at Papotech asked for this report. It compares his company with some competitors.

CONFIDENTIAL REPORT

Comparison of Papotech and its competitors

	Pay	Prices	Call centre	
	Average salary per month	Average price of most popular products	Number of phone staff per 1,000 customers	Average call time
Papotech	€1,420	€325	1.2	3 mins 45 secs
Office First	€1,830	€317	1.7	2 mins 30 secs
TMP	€1,560	€284	1.8	3 mins 10 secs

Work in groups. Read the report and discuss possible reasons for the problems.

***Example**: Staff probably leave because Papotech pays the lowest salaries.*

2 57▷ **The Director is discussing the report with a line manager. Listen and answer the questions.**

1 Which parts of the report do they discuss? What don't they discuss?
2 What reasons does the line manager give for the two problems?

3 57▷ **Listen again. Put phrases a–h into categories 1–4.**

a What's your opinion?
b In my opinion ...
c I think ...
d I agree.
e Do you think ...
f I don't think so.
g I'm not so sure.
h I think we should ...

1 Asking for an opinion: ___, ___
2 Giving an opinion: ___, ___, ___
3 Agreeing: ___
4 Disagreeing: ___, ___

» For more exercises, go to **Practice file 10** on page 96.

4 **Work with a partner. Discuss 1–4 below. Follow this model.**

A Ask B's opinion.
B Give your opinion.
A Agree or disagree.

1 Teams are always better than people working alone.
2 Meetings are never useful.
3 The best offer is usually the cheapest.
4 Employees prefer more pay than more training.

5 **Work in small groups. Look at the ideas in File 58 on page 117. Discuss what you should do to solve the problems at Papotech. You have a maximum budget of €200,000.**

ⓘ » Interactive Workbook » **Email** and » **Exercises and Tests**

Key expressions

Asking for an opinion
What do you think?
What's your opinion?
Do you think ...?

Giving an opinion
In my opinion ...
I think ... / I think we should ...
I don't think ...

Agreeing
Yes, I agree.
That's true.

Disagreeing
I disagree / don't agree.
I'm not so sure.

ⓘ » Interactive Workbook
» **Phrasebank**

Changing the way you work

Background

Team spirit

SEI is based in Pennsylvania. The building has no fixed offices, only office furniture on wheels so it can be moved to where someone wants it. This is to help people to work in teams. In fact, there are no levels of management, no secretaries – only team leaders and teams.

Some teams are permanent so they can work with an important client and offer a single contact for that client. Some teams get together to solve a temporary problem, and then stop when the job is finished. Employees can be members of two or three different teams. They do what they are good at, and sometimes they lead a team, sometimes they are a team member. The important thing is that they are flexible. They must also be happy to work on different projects at the same time and be well organized.

Discussion

1 **Do staff at SEI have their own offices?**

2 **How many teams do they work in?**

3 **Which roles do not exist at SEI?**

4 **Would you like to work in a company with this structure? Why / why not?**

5 **Do you think it is possible for your company to have this structure?**

Task

You work for a company with a similar structure to SEI. There are several new projects that need teams to work on them. Each project needs a team leader and some team members.

1 Next year's budgets.
2 A new brochure to advertise your services to companies.
3 A research project to look into possible new markets.
4 The annual staff party.

1 **Work with a partner. Talk about each project and the people they need.**
   1 What roles does each project need? Someone imaginative? Someone with marketing experience? A practical person?
   2 Which roles can you do? Why?
   3 Which projects would you like to work on?

2 **Now join another pair and share your ideas. Decide which of you are working on each project. How many projects are you working on? What other people do you need for each project?**

3 **Do you like this way of working? Is it an easy / successful way to work?**

11 | Travel

Learning objectives in this unit
- Talking about air travel
- Checking in at an airport
- Talking about future plans
- Giving reasons for actions
- Talking about money
- Staying at a hotel

Case study
- Organizing a business trip

Starting point

1 **Do you often travel on business? On holiday?**

2 **What is your favourite destination? Why?**

3 **What is the best way to travel?**

Working with words | Air travel

1 **When you travel by plane, which of these is most important to you? Number them 1 to 4. (1 = important, 4 = not important). Compare your answers with the rest of the class.**

Fast Internet access ___ Comfortable seating ___
No delays ___ Security ___

2 **Complete the headings in this text with the words in 1.**

Results from a survey: Business travel is boring!

In the past, business travel was cool and exciting. But interviews with 1,600 travellers show modern travel is stressful and boring.

1 ______________________
Nowadays, this rarely happens. Most modern travellers expect to be late. The problems start at **check-in**. There are long **queues** at **passport control** and the **gate**. Then if the planes aren't late, they can often be **cancelled**.

2 ______________________
Everyone agrees this is important, but the rules for **bags** and **hand luggage** are making journeys longer.

3 ______________________
47% do not get proper sleep. **Business class** helps, and the difference between a **window** or **aisle seat** can improve a journey, but more and more companies are saving money and choosing **economy class** for their employees.

4 ______________________
The successful business trip includes high-speed connections to the Internet at the airport **terminal** and hotel.

3 **Match the words in bold in the text in 2 to these definitions.**

1 Show your ticket and passport here and get your boarding card _check-in_
2 Get on the plane here ________
3 Show your passport here ________
4 Two types of ticket ________, ________
5 Pack this and carry it onto the plane ________
6 Pack these and check them in ________
7 Building where you arrive and leave ________
8 Lines of people ________
9 When the plane doesn't go ________
10 Two places to sit on the plane ________, ________

4 **Work with a partner and discuss these questions.**

1 What type of ticket and seat do you usually buy?
2 What was your worst journey? Give reasons (delays, long queues, etc.)

5 58▷ **Listen to this conversation at the check-in desk and look at this departure board. What is the flight number and destination?**

Destination	Flight	Time	Gate
London	BA227	0615	49b
Lima	BA655	0635	45
Hong Kong	BA335	0655	49

6 **Complete the conversation using some of the words from 3.**

A Hello, is this the [1]________ for all BA flights?
B Yes, it is. Do you have your passport and ticket?
A Here you are.
B And how many [2]________ are you checking in today?
A None. I just have [3]________.
B OK. Would you like a [4]________ or an [5]________ seat?
A Err, aisle please.
B OK. So your flight leaves from [6]________ 49 at 6.55, but boarding starts half an hour before. You're in [7]________ 5C.
A Thanks.

7 58▷ **Listen again and check.**

» For more exercises, go to **Practice file 11** on page 98.

8 **Work with a partner. Practise conversations at check-in using the information in the departures board above. Include these points in your conversations.**

- passport and ticket
- number of bags
- type of seat
- confirm flight details

9 **Work in small groups and discuss the difference in business travel between now and 5, 10, or 20 years ago.**

1 What is better now?
2 What is worse?

ⓘ » Interactive Workbook » **Glossary**

Language at work | *Going to* | Infinitive of purpose

1 Read this article and answer questions 1–4.

1 What problem do business travellers have?
2 What service does the company offer?
3 Where do they operate?
4 What are their plans?

Tour guides on the run

On your next business trip, **are you going to have** any time for sightseeing? Probably not. Even when it's a famous destination, most business travellers **aren't going to see** outside the airport, hotel, or conference room. But City Running Tours has the solution. Go for a run with a tour guide across the city and see all the local places of interest before breakfast. The company now offers tours of Charleston, Chicago, New York, San Diego, and Washington. It is now so popular with business travellers, that **they're going to offer** the service in even more cities in the future.

2 Look at the phrases in bold from the article in 1. Are they about the past, present, or future? Do they talk about a general plan or a specific arrangement?

3 Complete these rules.

1 Talk about general plans with *to be* + ________ + main verb.
2 In negative sentences, which part of the sentence changes: *to be? going to?* main verb?

4 Work with a partner. Take turns to ask and answer questions about plans for a business trip to Canada. Use the notes below.

Example: ***A*** *Are you going to have dinner with our colleagues?*
B *Yes, I am.*
A *Are you going to see Christophe?*
B *No, I'm not, but I'm going to meet Dominic.*

- have dinner with colleagues ✓
- see Christophe ✗ (meet Dominic)
- present new product ✓
- open new sales office ✓
- visit Ottawa office ✗ (visit Montreal)
- take train to Montreal ✓
- go sightseeing ✗ (no time)

Tip | *go* and *come*

Usually we use the present continuous (not *going to*) with the verbs *go* and *come*:
*We**'re going** to Toronto some time next month.*
NOT ~~*We're going to go to Toronto some time next month.*~~
*When **are you coming** back?*
NOT ~~*When are you going to come back?*~~

5 Work with a partner. Ask and answer questions about your next trip or holiday.

Are you I'm We're	going to	visit … open … have … see … offer … take … meet …

6 59▷ **Listen to this conversation with a business traveller about his next trip. Where is he going?**

7 59▷ **Listen again and match 1–4 to a–d.**

1 I'm going to visit Toronto first ___
2 I'm going to spend a day in Quebec ___
3 We're going out in the evening ___
4 I'm going to take Friday off ___

a ... **to present** the new product to Dominic and his team.
b ... **to see** the old city and have dinner.
c ... **to see** the sales reps there.
d ... **to have** a nice long weekend.

8 **Which form of the verb in 7 is in bold? Why is it used here? To say**

- why something happens?
- how something happens?
- when something happens?

» For more information and exercises, go to **Practice file 11** on page 99.

9 **Work with a partner. Make sentences about plans and the reason for them, using the prompts.**

Example: *I'm going to leave work early to go to the dentist.*

1 leave work early / go to the dentist
2 do a course / learn a new computer program
3 visit Delhi / see clients
4 ring Sashia / arrange a meeting
5 come to the office at the weekend / finish my report

10 **Write three plans for you or your company and explain the reason. Tell your partner about them.**

Practically speaking | How to talk about money

1 60▷ **Listen to three conversations about money and match them to these places.**

a bureau de change **b** taxi **c** airport shop

2 60▷ **How much money does the traveller pay or receive in each conversation?**

3 60▷ **Listen again and complete these sentences.**

1 How ________ is that?
2 Keep the ________.
3 Can I pay ________ credit card?
4 I'd like to ________ $500 ...
5 The exchange ________ is ...
6 What's the ________?

4 **Work with a partner. Role-play three situations using the information in these pictures.**

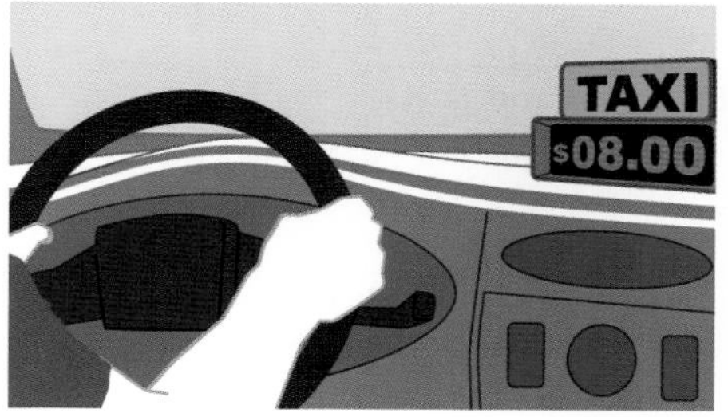

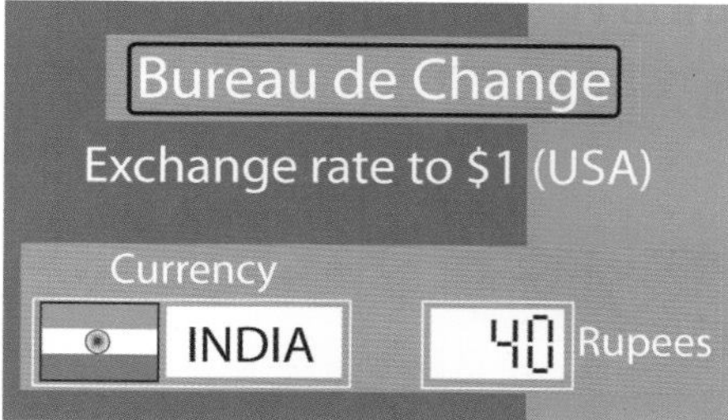

Business communication | Staying at a hotel

1 61▷ **Jenny Chiang is on a business trip in Dublin. She needs to book a hotel room. Work with a partner. Student A, turn to File 24 on page 109. Student B, turn to File 50 on page 115.**

2 61▷ **Tell each other your information then listen again and check.**

3 **Who says these expressions? The receptionist (*R*) or the visitor (*V*)?**

1 I'd like to book a room for the night. ___
2 Do you have any vacancies? ___
3 Does that include breakfast? ___
4 Can I have your name? ___
5 I need your credit card details. ___
6 What's the card number? ___
7 And the expiry date? ___
8 Where is the hotel exactly? ___

4 **Work with a partner. Student A, turn to File 25 on page 109. Student B, turn to File 51 on page 115.**

5 62▷ **Now listen to two more conversations at the hotel and answer these questions.**

1 What is Ms Chiang's room number?
2 What time is breakfast?
3 Does she need to book a table for dinner?
4 What two things does Ms Chiang want in the morning? At what time?
5 What two things does she want in her room?

6 62▷ **Complete these sentences with words from the list, then listen again and check.**

credit card *room* *table* *room service* *Internet access*
reservation *breakfast* *wake-up call*

1 I have a ______________ for tonight.
2 Can I see your ______________, please?
3 Your ______________ is on the fifth floor.
4 What time is ______________ served?
5 Do I need to book a ______________?
6 This is Ms Chiang in room 501. Can I have a ______________, please?
7 Do the rooms have ______________? I can't log on.
8 I'd also like dinner in my room. Do you have ______________?

» For more exercises, go to **Practice file 11** on page 98.

7 **Work with a partner. Student A, you are a hotel receptionist. Turn to File 59 on page 117 and answer questions about the services. Student B, turn to File 52 on page 115.**

8 **Change roles and repeat 7. Student B, turn to file 59 on page 117. Student A, turn to File 26 on page 109.**

ⓘ » Interactive Workbook » **Email** and » **Exercises and Tests**

Key expressions

Booking a room
I'd like a room for two nights.
Do you have any vacancies?
Does that include breakfast?
Can I book a room?

Checking in
I have a reservation.
Can I see your credit card, please?
Your room is …
What time is breakfast served?
Do I need to book a table for dinner?

Asking about services
Can I have a wake-up call?
Can you order me a taxi?
Do the rooms have Internet access?
Do you have room service?
Is there a gym / swimming pool / meeting room?

ⓘ » Interactive Workbook
» **Phrasebank**

Organizing a business trip

Background

The professionals' travel agent

Strand travel agents specializes in organizing business travel. They provide companies with a complete service from booking flights and train travel to getting passports and visas, as well as arranging evening entertainment and much more. They also search for locations for conferences and other events. Using a travel company to arrange all business travel means companies often get better prices for trips because the travel specialists have contacts that an individual company doesn't have, so they can often get cheaper deals.

Discussion

1 **Why do companies use Strand?**

2 **What are the advantages or disadvantages of this?**

Task

This company is planning a training event for its staff. It wants Strand to find some options for accommodation.

EuroStamp Sales Training – Istanbul.

A three-day training session for 30 sales staff from Central and Eastern Europe.

Presentations; Small group training sessions; Workshops

Evening entertainment – dinner on one evening and a tourist event on the other evening.

1 **Work with a partner. Student A, you work for Strand. You want to find out about Hotel Supreme. Call your partner and ask for the information below. Student B, you work at Hotel Supreme. Turn to file 27 on page 109.**

Hotel name	Hotel Excelsior	Hotel Orient	Hotel Supreme
Location	In the heart of Istanbul	Near the harbour	
Rooms available	15 double, 15 suites	10 double, 25 single	
Price	€200 double €300 suites Price includes breakfast	€225 double €175 single Breakfast €12	
Services	2 meeting rooms – 1 already reserved Chauffeur service	2 meeting rooms available 1 office with secretarial service Free transfer from airport	
Restaurant reservation	Restaurant closed for renovation	Yes – can reserve a table	
Special group booking rates	Yes – will send an offer	No special rates	

2 **You now work for EuroStamp. Compare, with your partner, the three hotels and decide which hotel is best for you.**

3 **Make an announcement to the staff about the choice you have made. Tell them what they are going to do and where they are going to stay.**

Case study

12 | Schedules

Learning objectives in this unit

- Talking about schedules
- Talking about recent past actions
- Saying when something happens
- Saying dates
- Planning a schedule

Activity

- The revision game

Starting point

1 **What's your busiest month?**

2 **Which month do you normally take a holiday in?**

3 **Which is your favourite season in the year? Spring, summer, autumn, or winter? Why?**

Working with words | Calendars and schedules

1 **These graphs show busy periods in the year for three types of business. Work with a partner and match the businesses to the graphs.**

delivering flowers *selling houses* *trade fair industry*

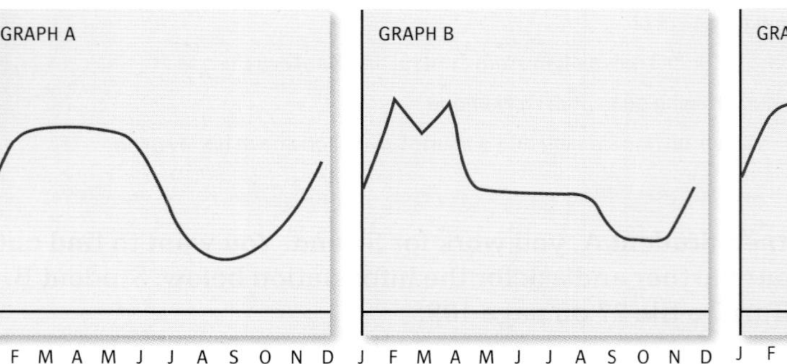

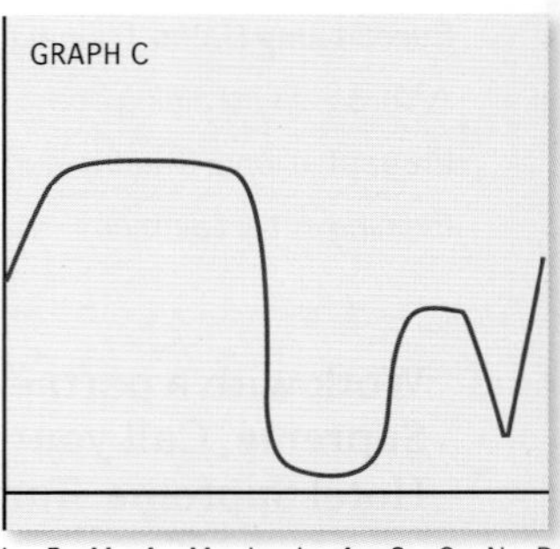

2 **Now read these texts from people working in these businesses. Check your answers in 1 and answer these questions.**

1. Which people have a similar schedule every year?
2. What is different about the real estate industry now?
3. Which days are very important in the flower delivery business?

Katrina Bieber works in the German Trade Fair Industry:
'60% of all major international trade fairs now take place in my country, and January to mid-May is the really busy period. So I can usually take my annual leave in June or July and then some more time off in the autumn before I start planning again for next year.'

Prescott Bowden runs a real estate firm in Atlanta, Georgia:
'People always think spring is a good time for selling houses, but you can't predict the market these days. For example, Christmas is the time when everyone has busy schedules, so you expect real estate to have a quiet period. But last year, December was one of our best months.'

Jayne Henry is a sales manager for a flower company:
'We promise to deliver flowers the same day so we have very tight deadlines. We also need to be sure we have the right amount of staff. For certain public holidays or Valentine's Day and Mother's Day we need about 80 people and five team leaders. During quiet weeks we only have about 10 full-time staff in the centre.'

3 **Find word pairs from the texts in 2 by matching a word from A to a word from B.**

A	B
tight ________	holiday
busy ________	period
annual ________	off
public ________	schedule
busy ________	period
quiet ________	deadline
time ________	leave

4 **Complete these questions with words from 3.**

1 Do you have a busy ________ and a ________ period during the day?
2 Do you have any time ________ this month? When is your annual ________?
3 Many companies have ________ deadlines around Christmas. Is this true for your company?
4 What happens if a ________ holiday is at the weekend?

5 **Work with a partner. Ask and answer the questions in 4.**

6 **Whose schedule is this from 2? Is she busy all week?**

Wednesday 27th	Thursday 28th	Friday 29th
Final day for annual conference registrations	10 a.m. Open trade fair stand	Day off – Long weekend in Paris!
8 p.m. Dinner with Franco at 'Nara Sushi' at Friesenstrasse 70	2 p.m. Meet association members	

Don't forget!
1 Email this timetable to Franco.
2 Email a reminder to members about Thursday meeting.

7 **Find four words or phrases in the schedule and note in 6 to match these definitions.**

1 time off on Saturday, Sunday and one extra day (Friday or Monday) ____________
2 a note to tell you to do something ____________
3 a plan or schedule with times for each stage ____________
4 meeting for a group of people once a year ____________

» For more exercises, go to **Practice file 12** on page 100.

8 **Work with a partner. Talk about the following.**

- your schedule or timetable this week
- deadlines this month
- time off and holidays this year
- events you have every year

Example: *I have a very busy schedule this week because …*

ⓘ » Interactive Workbook » **Glossary**

Tip | *remember, remind*

Remind *Katrina to send the schedule.* = Tell Katrina so she doesn't forget …

Katrina must ***remember*** *the schedule.* = Katrina mustn't forget …

Language at work | Present perfect

1 Greta Helsing works for Original Oils. Read the information about the company and her email below and answer these questions.

1 Where does Original Oils sell its product?
2 Where does it buy its materials?
3 What is Greta's deadline?

Original Oils imports and sells natural cosmetic products (soap, lotions) to high street shops in Western Europe. Usually, the company buys raw materials from Pakistan and India, but this year Original Oils **has ordered** Palmarosa oil from a new supplier in Nepal. It wants to produce a new soap with the oil for Valentine's day but the delivery **hasn't arrived yet**.

Subject: Palmarosa soap

Dear Barati
How are you? I'm checking our order because it hasn't arrived. **Have you shipped** the oil yet? We need the delivery by 20th October.
Greta Helsing
Original Oils

2 Look at the verbs in bold in 1 and answer these questions.

1 Are they talking / asking about a past, present, or future action?
2 Does the action affect the present or the past?

3 Complete these rules for forming the present perfect.

1 To make positive statements use have / ________ + past participle.
2 To make negative sentences use haven't / ________ + past participle.
3 To form the past participle of regular verbs (order, arrive, etc.) add ________ to the verb.

4 Work with a partner. Look at Barati's list. Take turns to say what he has or hasn't done.

Example: *He's checked the database.*

Check database (✓)
Contact shipping firm (✓)
Email producer (✓)
Telephone Greta (✗)
Arrange next visit to producers (✗)
Update website with product details (✓)

Tip | *yet*

With the negative and question form of the present perfect, you can add *yet* to say that you intend to do it:

*I haven't done it **yet** (but I'm going to ...)*

5 63▷ **Listen to this telephone call. Is the delivery going to be late? What is Greta going to change?**

6 63▷ **Listen again and complete these sentences with the present perfect of the verbs in brackets.**

1 We ____________________ (send) it …
2 We ____________________ (have) a few problems here.
3 ________ you ________ (take) lots of orders for the soap?
4 There ____________________ (be) a lot of interest.
5 ________ you ________ (see) some of the other products on our website?
6 ________ you ever ________ (be) to Nepal?

7 **Read the final part of audio 63 on page 127. How does Greta give short answers in the present perfect?**

» For more information and exercises, go to **Practice File 12** on page 101.

8 **Work with a partner. You each have some tasks to complete before the end of the week. Ask each other about your progress on the tasks. Student A, turn to File 28 on page 109. Student B, turn to File 53 on page 116.**

Practically speaking | How to use prepositions of time

1 **Underline the prepositions in these sentences.**

1 My busiest period is in spring.
2 My flight is at ten.
3 We open on public holidays.
4 I close the restaurant in May.
5 The conference starts on the thirteenth.
6 What are you doing at the weekend?

2 **Put the prepositions from 1 into this table.**

1 ________	2 ________	3 ________
… Monday	… February	… nine-thirty
… the twenty-first of November	… winter	… midday
… New Year's Day	… the morning	… the weekend
	… an hour	

3 **Tell your partner about these. Use a preposition of time.**

Example: *My birthday is on …*

- your birthday
- your annual leave
- your next trip abroad
- your busiest part of the year
- when this lesson ends

Business communication | Planning a schedule

Greta Helsing is meeting with Soledad and Martin at Original Oils. They are discussing and planning the schedule for the new Palmarosa Soap. Martin is coordinating production and Soledad deals with sales to the high street shops.

1 64▷ **Listen to the meeting. Complete Greta's notes with the dates.**

Palmarosa Soap	
Must be on the shelves by [1] ________.	Final product ready by [4] ________.
Launch date [2] ________	Start delivery to shops on [5] ________.
Packaging ready by [3] ________.	

2 64▷ **Listen again and match 1–12 to a–l to make sentences.**

1 … the schedule is ___
2 The situation is ___
3 … we've already ___
4 The aim is to ___
5 What's the deadline ___
6 What date is ___
7 We plan ___
8 How much time ___
9 Why don't we ___
10 Let's start ___
11 Is everyone happy ___
12 So, to summarize, I'm ___

a … taken it to the warehouse.
b … for this?
c … to launch it on January 20th.
d … deliver the product …?
e … get the soap on the shelves …
f … with that date?
g … do we need for production?
h … about a week late.
i … delivery from the warehouse …
j … going to call our packaging people
k … that the raw material from Nepal has just arrived.
l … the launch?

3 **Put the sentences in 2 into these categories.**

1 Stating the current situation: ___, ___, ___
2 Saying what needs to be done: ___, ___
3 Asking about dates and times: ___, ___, ___
4 Proposing a plan: ___, ___
5 Summarizing and confirming the plan: ___, ___

» For more exercises, go to **Practice file 12** on page 100.

4 **Work in groups of three. You are preparing a company brochure for next year. Today's date is July 1st.**
Student A is in charge of the schedule. Turn to File 33 on page 111.
Student B is in charge of information for the brochure and dealing with the designers. Turn to File 54 on page 116.
Student C is dealing with the printers. Turn to File 57 on page 116.

5 **Present your schedule to another group. How similar are your schedules?**

6 **Make a list of the stages in a typical schedule where you work.**
For example:

- invoicing customers each month
- arranging the weekly staff meeting
- the stages for a new product
- arranging the annual conference

Present the stages to the class and say how long each stage usually takes.

ⓘ » Interactive Workbook » **Email** and » **Exercises and Tests**

Key expressions

Stating the current situation
At the moment, the schedule …
The situation is that …
We've already …

Saying what needs to be done
The aim is to …
We plan to …

Asking about dates and times
What's the deadline?
What date …?
How much time do we need for …?

Proposing a plan
What if …?
Let's …
Why don't we …?

Summarizing / confirming the plan
Is everyone happy with that date?
I'm / You're / We're going to …
So, to summarize …

ⓘ » Interactive Workbook
» **Phrasebank**

The revision game

Work with a partner. Take turns to choose a square.

On a yellow square, have a role-play with your partner, on a blue square follow the instruction, on a pink square answer the question(s).
If you are correct, or if you complete the role-play, you win the square.
If you are not correct, the squares stays open.
The winner is the first person to win five squares in a row, across (➡), down (⬇), or diagonally (↘).

Questions: Where are you from? What is your nationality? What is your job?	**Instruction:** Find the mistake: Are you from Peru? Yes, I from.	**Question:** When you take a flight, what's the procedure at the airport?	**Instruction:** Explain how to use the photocopier.	**Instruction:** Talk about your last phone call. Who was it with? What was it about?
Phone call: **A** Call a hotel and ask about its services then book a room. **B** Answer B's questions.	**Questions:** Which words go together? tight / leave / annual / schedule / busy / deadline	**Conversation:** **A** Introduce yourself to B – you've never met. **B** Respond.	**Instruction:** Compare your company to its competitors.	**Questions:** Can I join you? Do you come here often? What do you think of this lesson?
Instruction: Ask your partner three questions about his / her job.	**Meeting:** Give your opinion on this then ask for B's opinion: Your CEO wants to move your offices to a city 500 km away.	**Instruction:** Talk about your job and your responsibilities.	**Question:** What's your company working on at the moment?	**Phone call:** **A** You want to speak to a colleague but he / she isn't there. Leave a message. **B** Answer the call.
Phone call: **A** Call your partner and ask for his / her email address. **B** Respond.	**Question:** What have you done today?	**Question:** What is the location of your company and what is near it?	**Instruction:** Think of three qualities that these jobs need: • airline pilot • administrator	**Question:** What do you do if you work in real estate?
Instruction: Describe your favourite restaurant using superlatives, e.g. *best*, *most expensive*, etc.	**Meeting:** Plan a party for your English group next week. Discuss with B your plan and the schedule.	**Instruction:** Describe a typical day at work. Use these words: *always*, *often*, *rarely*, *sometimes*, *usually*, and *never*	**Questions:** Where is your head office? What other workplaces does your company have?	**Instruction:** Give a visitor to your company directions from Reception to your office.
At a hotel: **A** Arrive at a hotel and check in. Ask about breakfast and dinner. **B** Respond.	**Instruction:** Talk about your last trip. Where did you go? How long? When did you leave / arrive?	**Questions:** What are your plans for the next year / few months? Why are you doing this?	**Phone call:** **A** Call and arrange a meeting for next week. **B** Respond.	**Instruction:** Ask for help to print a document.

1 Practice file

Working with words

1 Match products 1–8 to their nationalities a–h.

1 Coca Cola ___
2 De Beer diamonds ___
3 British Airways airline ___
4 Sanyo electronics ___
5 LOT airline ___
6 Andhra Rice ___
7 Fiat cars ___
8 Cachaca rum ___

a American
b Indian
c Japanese
d British
e Polish
f Brazilian
g South African
h Italian

2 Complete this chart with a job from the list that works for or with these people.

Technician
Sales Rep
Human Resources
Personal Assistant
Receptionist
Financial Director
Team Leader

Managing Director	1 P________ A________
Sales Director	2 S________ R________
3 F________ D________	bookkeepers
4 H________ R________ Manager	Training Officer 5 T________ L________;
Production Manager	6 T________
Facilities Manager	7 R________

3 Read these business cards and complete the business person's profile.

Haruo Ogawa
FINANCIAL DIRECTOR
TOYOTA **JAPAN**

I'm 1________ (name).
I'm from 2________ (country)
and I'm a 3________ (job).
My company is 4________ (nationality).

Isadora De Souza
Receptionist
PETROBRAS
BRAZIL

Her name is 5________.
She's 6________ (nationality).
She's a 7________ (job). Her company is in 8________ (country).

Jade Botha **TEAM LEADER**
SA Airlink
SOUTH AFRICA

I'm 9________ (name).
I'm from 10________ (country)
and I'm a 11________ (job).
My company is 12________ (nationality).

Business communication

1 Put these conversations in the right order.

1 a ___ I'm fine. This is my colleague, Martin Altenberg.
b ___ Hello. Pleased to meet you, Gundula. How are you?
c ___ How do you do, Martin?
d ___ Hello. My name's Gundula Bauer.

2 a ___ No. How do you do? I'm Stefani.
b ___ Do you know Ariadne?
c ___ And you.
d ___ Pleased to meet you, Stefani.

3 a ___ Thanks. Nice meeting you and your colleague.
b ___ Bye.
c ___ Yes, have a good journey.
d ___ It's time to leave. See you soon.
e ___ Goodbye.

2 Underline the best option in *italics*.

A [1]*This is Pietre. / How are you?* He's my assistant.
B [2]*How do you do? / Nice to meet you too.* Pleased to meet you.
A [3]*I'm fine. / And you.*

C [4]*Do you know Franziska? / How do you do?*
D Yes! [5]*I'm fine. / It's good to see you again.*
C Yes, you too. [6]*Nice meeting you. / How are you?*
D I'm fine. And you?

E Good morning. I have an appointment with Ms Cernoskova. [7]*This is / My name's* Ludmilla Osimk.
F [8]*How do you do? / It's good to see you again.* I'm Timo, Ludmilla's assistant.
E Oh, [9]*nice to meet you. / have a good journey.*

3 Complete this conversation with phrases from the list.

Nice meeting you
Do you know
my name's
see you soon
Bye
Have a good journey
How do you do?
Nice to meet you

A Hello, 1________ Geraldine.
B Hi. 2________. I'm Vincenz.
A 3________ Alessandro, my colleague?
B No. How do you do?
C 4________ Nice to meet you.
…
C Our flight leaves soon. 5________, Vincenz.
B Yes, nice meeting you too. 6________.
A Bye, and 7________.
B 8________.

Language at work | *To be* | Possessives

To be

Form

Positive:

I	am / 'm	a receptionist.
You / We / They	are / 're	Polish.
He / She / It	is / 's	from Brazil.

Negative:

I	am not / 'm not	a team leader.
You / We / They	are not / aren't	Italian.
He / She / It	is not / isn't	from South Africa.

Questions:

Am	I	a Personal Assistant?
Are	you / we / they	Brazilian?
Is	he / she / it	from Italy?

Short answers:

Yes,	I	am.
	you / we / they	are.
	he / she / it	is.
No,	I	'm not.
	you / we / they	aren't.
	he / she / it	isn't.

A ***Are you*** *a Financial Director?* *B* *No,* ***I'm not****.* ***I'm a*** *receptionist.*

A ***Is he*** *a Technician?* *B* *Yes,* ***he is****.*

A ***Are they*** *Team Leaders?* *B* *No,* ***they aren't****.* ***They're*** *Personal Assistants.*

A ***Is it*** *an American product?* *B* *Yes,* ***it is****.*

Possessives

Form

I → my
you → your
he → his
she → her
it → its
we → our
they → their

Use

To say who has or owns something.

I have a personal assistant. Greta is ***my*** *personal assistant.*
Jonas has a company car. ***His*** *car is a BMW.*
We have a good team. ***Our*** *team is very small.*

1 Complete these sentences, questions, and answers.

1 ______ he Italian?
No, he ______. He's Japanese.
2 ______ they Italian?
No, they ______. They ______ Polish.
3 ______ Mirelle Brazilian?
Yes, she ______.
4 The company ______ South African, it's British.
5 We ______ in Warsaw, in Poland.
6 ______ they Technicians?
Yes, they ______.
7 ______ you a Personal Assistant?
Yes, I ______.
8 ______ Awad the CEO?
No, he ______. He ______ the Financial Director.

2 Underline the correct word in *italics*.

1 This is my department – Customer Service. Lawrie is *my / his* boss.
2 She has an assistant and *her / my* name is Pauline.
3 *Your / You* desk is next to Pauline's.
4 Next to you is Harald and those are *her / his* biscuits on his desk from a client.
5 The coffee machine is for *our / their* office only – not the whole department.
6 They have *their / my* coffee machine in the HR kitchen.

3 Complete this email with the words from the list.

am   your   my   our   are (x2)   is (x3)   her

Subject: my new company

Hi Abdul,
Here's the information about us:
The name of the company is IT-express. It [1] ______ a computer company. I [2] ______ the CEO, and my four colleagues [3] ______ the technicians. Pascale is [4] ______ personal assistant.
[5] ______ office is in Tunis but the customers [6] ______ in Spain.
Yolanda [7] ______ the new sales rep. She [8] ______ Spanish but [9] ______ French and English are very good.
Send me [10] ______ phone number so we can meet.

Regards
Kashyar

Working with words

1 Match 1–4 to a–d, then 5–7 to e–g to make sentences.

1 We employ ___
2 We export to ___
3 We produce ___
4 Customers buy ___

a … the Asian market.
b … our financial services from banks.
c … 6,000 people at our company, worldwide.
d … electronic components for computers.

5 We provide ___
6 We sell ___
7 We develop ___

e … new technology for telecommunications.
f … training for our software.
g … our products to supermarkets.

2 Complete this crossword.

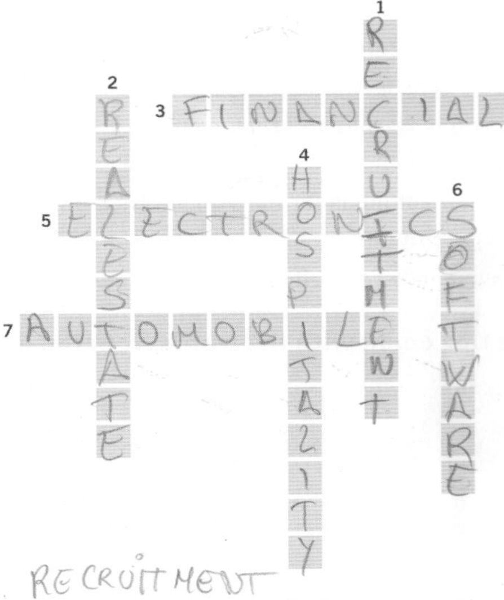

1 A ___ company finds new employees.
2 This company sells houses and offices. (4, 6)
3 Banks provide us with ___ services.
4 Hotels and restaurants are in the ___ industry.
5 Samsung is an ___ company.
6 Microsoft produces this.
7 Car production is part of the ___ industry.

Business communication

1 Put this conversation in the right order.

a ___ Hello. Can I book two meeting rooms at your hotel for March 10th please?
b ___ Good morning. Holiday Lodge. How can I help you?
c ___ Yes, of course. Can you give me your company name, please?
d ___ Sorry, can you say that again, please?
e ___ Yes, it's BHH Plastics. Can you give me the prices please?
f ___ Yes, one small meeting room costs …
g ___ Yes. We have one small meeting room for €120 a day and the large conference room costs €200.

2 Put the words in *italics* in the right order to complete the conversation from 1.

B Thanks. *Can / me / you / a / special / give / price* [1] ___ for two rooms?
A *I'm / don't / but / sorry / we* [2] ___ give special prices for one day, but I can speak to the manager about it.
B OK, thanks. Do you have Internet access in the meeting rooms?
A *Yes / do / we* [3] ___.
B Good. *Can / confirm / you* [4] ___ my booking by email, please?
A Sure. *Can / me / give / you* [5] ___ your email address?
B It's Rafael.lemand@bhh.com.
A *Can / that / spell / you* [6] ___?
B Yes, r-a-f-a-e-l, dot, l-e-m-a-n-d, at bhh dot com.
A Thank you.

3 Choose the best answer from a or b.

1 MMW. Can I help you?
a Hello. Can I order two laptops, please?
b Can you tell me your name, please?

2 Can you give me the prices, please?
a Can you spell that?
b Yes, of course.

3 Can you confirm by email, please?
a Sure, can you give me your email address?
b Can you speak more slowly?

4 My name's Wiktoria Poslavski.
a Sure.
b Can you spell that, please?

5 My phone number's 08392739.
a I'm sorry, but we don't do that.
b Can you speak more slowly, please?

Language at work | Present simple

Present simple

Form

Positive:

Subject + verb

*They **work** for Vodafone.*
*She **works** for Vodafone.*

Negative:

Subject + *do* / *does not* + verb

*I **don't** / **do not** work for IBM.*
*He **doesn't** / **does not** work for IBM.*

Questions:

Do / *Does* + subject + verb?

***Do** I / you / we / they work for Unilever?*

***Does** he / she / it work for Unilever?*

Short answers:

Yes / *No* + subject + *do* / *does* / *don't* / *doesn't*.

*Yes, I **do**.*
*Yes, he **does**.*
*No, they **don't**.*
*No, it **doesn't**.*

Careful: *he* / *she* / *it*: No *-s* on main verb in negative and question forms.

Spelling

Most verbs: *He* / *she* / *it* + verb + *-s*

He works, imports, sells, buys

Verbs ending in *-o*, *-ch*, *-ss*, *-sh*, *-x*: *He* / *she* / *it* + verb + *-es*

She goes, watches, misses, washes, fixes

Verbs with consonant + *-y*: replace the *-y* with *-ies*

Apply → he applies, try → she tries, fly → it flies

Exceptions: *Have → has*

Use

To talk about general facts.

*Glaxo **produces** pharmaceutical products.*
*BMW **doesn't provide** financial services.*
***Do** you **produce** electronics? **No, I don't. I work** in the service industry.*

1 **Complete these questions with the verb in brackets. Then add a short answer.**

1 A ________ you ________ your products to France? (export)
  B Yes, we ________.
2 A ________ they ________ for GM? (work)
  B Yes, they ________.
3 A ________ Remax ________ real estate? (sell)
  B Yes, it ________.
4 A ________ she ________ training for managers? (provide)
  B No, she ________.
5 A ________ we ________ more than 10 nationalities in our company? (employ)
  B Yes, we ________.
6 A ________ you ________ products from your country? (buy)
  B No, I ________.

2 **Complete the email below with the correct form of the verbs from the list.**

employ have produce work (not) sell export (not)

To: Klaudia@bme.cz
From: s.field@bme.com
Subject: New customer information

Hello Klaudia,
Here's some information about your new customer:
The company [1]________ computer components.
It [2]________ 800 people in Europe. Its head office is in Toulouse. It [3]________ to America, but it [4]________ to most of Asia. We [5]________ with their offices in the UK, but we [6]________ contact with their factories in France and Italy.
Good luck with your meeting on Tuesday.
Sandy

3 **Correct the mistakes.**

1 You do work for Terranova? ________
2 We imports most of our products. ________
3 Nokia doesn't works in the automobile industry.
____
4 Does Jane work for HSBC? Yes, she do.
____
5 Do you work in the recruitment industry?
Yes, I work. ________
6 Max doesn't develops software. He provides software training. ________
7 Your company employs 500 people? ________

3 | Practice file

Working with words

1 Match countries a–l to the regions they are located in.

1 Latin America ___, ___
2 Europe ___, ___
3 North America ___, ___
4 Africa ___, ___
5 The Middle East ___, ___
6 Asia-Pacific ___, ___

a Iran
b France
c Colombia
d Morocco
e Peru
f Australia
g Qatar
h Singapore
i The United States
j Canada
k Hungary
l Botswana

2 Complete the text with words from the list.

distribution centres factories sales offices
technical centre head office

I work for an international company. Our [1]___________ is in Sweden – that's where the management works. Our reps work from 30 [2]___________ around the world, but we only have six [3]___________ for our stock. We make the products in the Far East – our [4]___________ are in China, but our main [5]___________ is in India – this is where we develop new products.

3 Match the words from 2 to these definitions.

1 We make our products here. ___________
2 This is where we test the products and do research and development. ___________
3 When our sales reps aren't with a customer, they work here. ___________
4 The management department of the company works here. ___________
5 We deliver the products to customers from this location. ___________

Business communication

1 Who says these phrases, the caller (*C*) or the receiver (*R*)?

1 Can she call me back? ___
2 Can I take a message? ___
3 My number is 759 3810. ___
4 Can I have a contact number? ___
5 Could I leave a message? ___
6 I'd like to speak to Lena-Maria, please. ___
7 I'm sorry, but he isn't here today. ___
8 I'll give him your message. ___

2 Complete this dialogue with questions from the list.

Can I take a message? Can I have a contact number?
Can she call me back? So that's 0747 58360?
Is Galina there, please?

A Jocelyn speaking. Can I help you?
B Hi. [1]___________
A I'm sorry, but she isn't available. [2]___________
B Yes, please. I'm calling about our order. [3]___________
A Sure. [4]___________
B Yes, it's 07747 58360. The name's Tiernan.
A [5]___________
B No, it's 077 – double 7.

3 Put the words in *italics* in the correct order to complete the dialogue.

A ADAC. Good morning.
B Hello. *Could / I / to / speak* [1]___________ Adira Chen, please?
A *I'm / she's / but / sorry* [2]___________ in a meeting.
B Oh. *Could / leave / a / I / message* [3]___________?
A Sure.
B My name's Vrajkishore Kundu and my number is 08274 38573. *Can / back / call / me / she* [4]___________ as soon as possible?
A So that's Mr Kundu, telephone number 08274 38573. *Is / right / that* [5]___________?
B That's right.
A *I'll / message / her / give / your* [6]___________.

Language at work | *There is / are* | *Some / any*

There is / are

There is / there's / there is not / there isn't + singular noun

There's a factory in Beijing.
There isn't an office in Africa.

There are / there are not / there aren't + plural noun

There are factories all over the world.
There aren't any offices in Asia and Europe.

Questions:
Invert *is / are* and *there*.

Is there a factory in America?
Are there offices in Croatia?

Short answers:
Don't repeat the subject.

A Is there an office in Bahrain? *B Yes, there is.*
A Are there a lot of employees? *B No, there aren't.*

Some / any

Use *some / any* with plural nouns.

Some in positive sentences

*There are **some products** in the distribution centre.*

Any in negative sentences and questions

*There **aren't any products** in the sales office.*
***Are there any managers** in the technical centre?*

1 Read this information and complete the questions and answers.

In Cairo Conference & Exhibition Center	Near to Conference & Exhibition Center
1200 parking spaces	Shops
Chinese garden	Banks
3 large meeting rooms	5-star hotels
Restaurants	Airport

1 Are there any restaurants in the Conference Center?
Yes, ________________.
2 Are there any shops in the Conference Center?
________________.
3 ________________ hotels near the Conference Center?
4 Is there a bank in the Conference Center?
________________.
5 ________________ meeting rooms?
________________.
6 ________________ parking spaces?
7 Is there an airport near the Conference Center?
________________.

2 Complete this email with *some / any* or *a / an*.

Dear Brioni,

Our visitors arrive on Thursday. Please check we have everything ready.

FOOD:
There are [1]________ drinks in the meeting room – are there [2]________ biscuits?
There aren't [3]________ sandwiches for lunch, but there is [4]________ restaurant near the office.

MEETING ROOMS:
There's [5]________ video projector and [6]________ pens and paper. There isn't [7]________ laptop and there isn't [8]________ wireless connection.

ARRIVING:
Are there [9]________ parking spaces in the car park for them? There are [10]________ name cards for them and [11]________ info pack about the company at Reception.

Thanks
J

3 Tick (✓) the correct sentence, a or b.

1 a There are three factories in Europe and one in Asia.
  b There's three factories in Europe and one in Asia.
2 a There aren't any sales reps in China.
  b There are any sales reps in China.
3 a There are some managers in the technical centre and some in head office.
  b There is some managers in the technical centre and some in head office.
4 a There isn't some distribution centre in Britain.
  b There isn't a distribution centre in Britain.
5 a There isn't any sales office in Dubai.
  b There isn't a sales office in Dubai.
6 a Are there a computer programmer here?
  b Are there any computer programmers here?
7 a Is there a receptionist in the technical centre? Yes, there are.
  b Is there a receptionist in the technical centre? Yes, there is.
8 a Is there a car park at the distribution centre? Yes, there isn't.
  b Is there a car park at the distribution centre? No, there isn't.

Working with words

1 Complete these instructions with words from the list.

battery screen button
username and password start menu

1 Touch the ________________ to choose your options.
2 Enter your ________________ and you are connected.
3 For 25 copies, key in 25 and press the green ________________.
4 Can I recharge my ________________ here? I need to make a call.
5 Click on the ________________ and go to Settings.

2 Match the instructions in 1 to the equipment.

a Laptop __
b mobile phone __
c photocopier __
d ticket machine __
e wireless connection __

3 Match 1–7 to a–g to complete these instructions.

1 To make a coffee, fill it with water and switch __
2 To get money from your bank account, insert your card and key __
3 To book the flight, log __
4 To find the document, click __
5 Don't forget to switch __
6 At the hotel, put __
7 You need a password to connect __

a … in your personal number.
b … off the photocopier when you've finished.
c … on the icon 'open file'.
d … on the machine.
e … in your card to open the bedroom door.
f … to our network.
g … on to the website and find the flight you want.

4 Underline the correct words in *italics*.

1 *Touch / Insert / Key in* your credit card, then *key in / push / touch* the screen and choose your ticket.
2 *Switch on / Log on / Click on* your PC and *touch / connect / enter* your username.
3 *Touch / Click on / Switch off* the icon, then *connect / key in / insert* to the Internet.
4 *Log on to / Enter / Press* the green button to make the copies.

Business communication

1 Complete these four conversations.

A Can you [1]g________ m________ a h________?
B Sure.
A I [2]d________ k________ h________ t________ put these photos onto CD-ROM. I'm [3]t________ t________ copy them for Bob.

C Can you [4]h________ m________?
D Yes, [5]o________ c________.
C [6]H________ d________ I send a file to Sandy?
D Let me see.

E Do you [7]w________ a h________?
F That [8]w________ b________ g________. I don't know how to log on.

G I'm trying to download a document.
H Can I [9]h________?
G Oh, [10]y________, p________.
H Click on that icon and …

2 Put these dialogues in the right order.

A
a __ Sure.
b __ I've got a problem. I'm trying to book a flight on the Internet, but it doesn't work.
c __ John, can you help me?
d __ Yes, but I don't know how to enter it.
e __ Do you have a username for the website?
f __ Click on here, then key it in.

B
a __ That would be good.
b __ What's the problem?
c __ How do I print this document?
d __ Let me see …
e __ Are you OK Galina? Do you want a hand?

3 Underline the best response in *italics*.

1 A Do you want a hand?
B *That would be good. / Yes, of course.*
2 A Can you give me a hand?
B *Yes, please. / Sure.*
3 A Can you help me?
B *Yes, of course. / That would be good.*
4 A Can I help?
B *Yes, of course. / Yes, please.*

Language at work | Adverbs of frequency | Questions

Adverbs of frequency

Form

The adverb of frequency goes **before** the main verb.

*I **never work** 10 hours a day.*
*He **always takes** a break.*

The adverb of frequency goes **after** the verb *be*.

*I **am never** late.*
*He **is always** late.*
*You **are sometimes** sick.*

Use

To describe how often / regularly someone does something.

never rarely sometimes often usually always

0% ● —— 50% —— ● 100%

Questions (present simple)

Form

Question word + *do* / *does* + subject + verb phrase.

Who do you work for?
What does she do?
Where do they live?

See also **Practice file 2** for other question forms in the present simple.

Meaning

To ask about:

The way / method
***How** do you travel to work? By train.*

People / the company you work for
***Who** does she work for? Philips.*

General information
***What** do they do? They sell electronics.*

Frequency
***How often** does he take a holiday? Once a year.*

A place
***Where** do you work? In Singapore.*

The reason
***Why** do they like the company? The pay is very good.*

A time
***When** do we start work? At 8.00.*

1 This chart shows the number of days the employees were late for work last month. Complete the sentences about the employees using the words in the list.

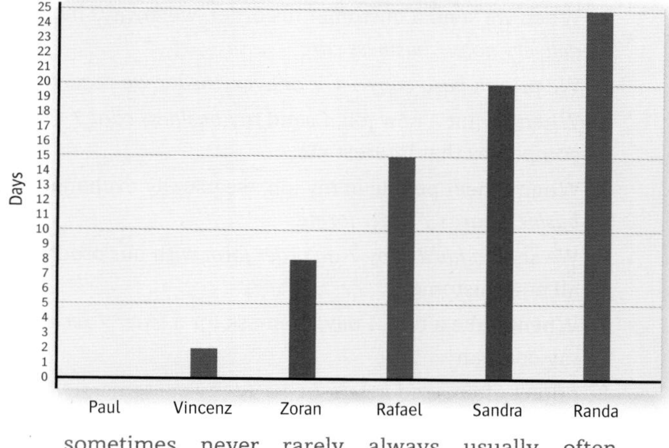

sometimes never rarely always usually often

1 Paul is ________ late for work.
2 Sandra is ________ late for work.
3 Zoran is ________ late for work.
4 Vincenz is ________ late for work.
5 Randa is ________ late for work.
6 Rafael is ________ late for work.

2 Put the words in *italics* in the right order.

1 *She / break / takes / always / a*
________________ at 10 o'clock.
2 *We're / sick / rarely* ________________.
3 *They / never / seven / days / work*
________________ a week.
4 *I / off / take / usually / Friday* ________________.
5 *We / finish / work / sometimes*
________________ at 16.00.
6 *He's / late / for / work / often* ________________.

3 Match questions 1–6 to answers a–f.

1 When do you have lunch? ___
2 How often do you go to work by train? ___
3 What does your company do? ___
4 Who do you work with? ___
5 Where do you take a break? ___
6 Why do you like your job? ___

a I usually go to the canteen for a coffee.
b At 12 o'clock.
c It's very interesting.
d Never, I always drive.
e I have three colleagues in my team.
f It develops software.

Working with words

1 Underline the correct word in *italics*.

1 We receive *a letter / an invoice* every month for the products we buy.
2 When we send a customer his order, we always include a *delivery note / business card.*
3 We print a *hard copy / CV* of every order we receive.
4 When I want a new job, I send my *business card / CV* to companies that interest me.
5 When I meet people in my job, we usually exchange *business cards / order forms.*
6 We send *a hard copy / an order form* with our brochure to all new customers.
7 When I take a taxi, I pay, then ask for a *letter / receipt* for my company.
8 I don't often send *letters / CVs* to my customers. We communicate by email.

2 Complete this email with words from the list.

save print receive open send forward

To: José_Pablo@blc.com
From: Tiler.macintyre@blc.com
Subject: organizing paperwork / PC problems!

Hello José
There are a few IT problems in our office today, so can you do me a favour?

Can you [1]__________ a hard copy of the report from the meeting and give it to Amanda? I also need a copy - can you [2]__________ the document to me in your next email?

Also, I can't [3]__________ our customer correspondence folder. If you can, please [4]__________ the order forms in this folder.

Can you [5]__________ me the invoice from Bertrands so I have their contact details, please?

Finally, can you call me when you [6]__________ this email? I don't know if my email is working!

Thanks,
T

3 ~~Cross out~~ the verb a, b, or c that *doesn't* match with the noun.

	a	b	c	
1	a receive	b attach	c print	an email
2	a receive	b print	c open	a business card
3	a forward	b print	c receive	a hard copy
4	a open	b attach	c print	a folder

Business communication

1 Complete these conversations with phrases from the lists.

A

You need to
There are some problems with
explain the situation
I'll speak to
That would be great

A [1]__________ the equipment and the products aren't ready for the Polish order. Can you help?
B [2]__________ contact the customer and [3]__________.
A OK.
B [4]__________ the service engineers.
A [5]__________.

B

We did, but
for your help
I'll explain
I'll call
No problem
You need to
We can't

A [6]__________ find the invoice for Delaney & Co. They want a special price.
B [7]__________ call Jenny in the Accounts department.
A [8]__________ she wasn't in the office.
B [9]__________ the customer then. Do they normally have a special price?
A No, not usually.
B OK. [10]__________ the situation.
A That's great. Thanks a lot [11]__________.
B [12]__________.

2 Complete these phrases and find the hidden message.

1 We n _ _ _ to fix the problem.
2 Don't w _ _ _ _.
3 I'll e _ _ _ _ _ _ the situation.
4 That would be g _ _ _ _
5 We've got a _ _ _ _ _ _ _ with the order.
6 I'll c _ _ _ the customer now.
7 We c _ _ _ deliver in time.
8 We changed the software, but it d _ _ _ _ work.
9 I'll let you know as soon as I _ _ _.

Language at work | Past simple: *be* and regular verbs

Past simple: *be*

Form

Positive: Subject + *was / were* …

*I / He / She / It **was** at the presentation.*
*You / We / They **were** at the presentation.*

Negative: Subject + *was not (wasn't) / were not (weren't)* …

*I / He / She / It **wasn't** in the office.*
*You / We / They **weren't** in the office.*

Questions: (Question word*) + *was / were / wasn't / weren't* + subject …?

***Was she** in the office?*
***Why weren't you** at work?*

Past simple: regular verbs

Form

Positive: Subject + verb+-*ed* …

*I **worked** for Vodafone.*
*They **talked** about branding.*

Negative: Subject + ***did not / didn't*** + verb …

*They **didn't like** the presentation.*
*You **did not ask** any questions.*

Questions: (Question word*) + *did / didn't* + subject + verb …?

***Did** she **work** for Unilever?*
***When did** you **leave** your last job?*

Short answers: Don't repeat the main verb.

*A Did she work for Unilever? B Yes, she **did**.*

*See Practice file 4 for question words.

Spelling

Most regular verbs: verb + -*ed*

start → *started*

Verbs ending in -*e*: verb + -*d*

decide → *decided*

Verbs ending in consonant-vowel-consonant: double the last letter + -*ed*

stop → *stopped*

Verbs ending in consonant + -*y*: replace -*y* with -*ied*

try → *tried*

Use

To talk about a finished action in the past. We usually know when the action / event happened or didn't happen.

*I **was** at the meeting last week.*
*I **received** your message yesterday.*
*You **didn't send** me the document.*

To ask when an action in the past took place.

*When **did** the conference **start**?*

1 Underline the correct word in *italics*.

A How [1]*was / were* the meeting?

B I don't know, I [2]*wasn't / weren't* there. I [3]*was / were* on holiday, but John emailed me the notes from the meeting. It [4]*was / were* very long!

A I'm glad I [5]*were / was* off sick then! Remi and Anna [6]*were / was* also away. They [7]*were / was* on a skiing holiday, but there [8]*wasn't / weren't* any snow!

2 Put the words in 1–5 in the right order to make questions, then match them to answers a–e.

1 they / weren't / why / the / at / meeting
______?

2 interesting / was / it
______?

3 questions / were / many / there
______?

4 was / last / your / when / business trip
______?

5 at / who / the / meeting / was
______?

a Yes, it was. ___
b Last Friday. ___
c They were in Los Angeles. ___
d Max and Yolanda. ___
e No, there weren't. ___

3 Complete this text with the past simple form of the verbs in brackets.

Report: Seminar Hotel Booking

We [1]______ (decide) to use Travel Inn. I [2]______ (call) to ask for a special price and they [3]______ (email) me back to say it [4]______ (not be) possible. We [5]______ (not contact) them again and [6]______ (try) another hotel. Two days later, we [7]______ (receive) an email from Travel Inn. They [8]______ (be) sorry about the prices and [9]______ (offer) us a 10% discount. I [10]______ (book) the meeting room immediately and they [11]______ (confirm) this in writing. It [12]______ (be) exactly what we [13]______ (want).

4 Make questions in the past simple using the prompts.

1 When / you / start work? ______
2 Where / she / go on holiday? ______
3 Why / you / not email / me? ______
4 How / you / contact her? ______
5 Who / they / speak to? ______
6 Why / we / not call / him? ______

Working with words

1 Complete this menu with words from the list.

Main course   order   Dessert
side salad   Dish   courses
Starter

Two [1]________ for only €12.00 or three for €15.00

[2]________
Tomato soup
Avocado salad
Antipasti selection

[3]________ ________
Chicken casserole
Spaghetti bolognese
Grilled tuna steak

[4]________
Summer fruits and ice cream
Chocolate mousse
Apple strudel and cream

[5]________ of the day
Fish pie made with local fish
Served with a [6]________
____

Please [7]________ at the bar

2 Complete these sentences with *a*, *an*, or *some*.

1 I'd like ________ glass of still water, please.
2 Would you like ________ vegetables with that?
3 Could I have ________ side salad with my steak, please?
4 I'll have ________ avocado salad, please.
5 We'd like ________ extra portion of French fries, please.
6 Could I have ________ parmesan cheese, please?
7 Would you like ________ starter?
8 I'll have ________ glass of red wine, please.

3 Put these conversations in the right order.

A a ___ Would you like a side dish with that?
b ___ Yes, I'll have a four seasons pizza, please.
c ___ Are you ready to order?
d ___ No problem.
e ___ No thanks, but I'd like a glass of red wine, please.

B a ___ How was your meal?
b ___ Would you like a dessert?
c ___ And could I have the bill, please?
d ___ Sure.
e ___ No thank you, but we'd like two coffees, please.
f ___ Very nice, thanks.

Business communication

1 Underline the correct phrase in *italics* to complete the conversation.

A Hello, I'm Rachel, [1]*Can I join you? / Can I help you?*
B [2]*Yes, of course. / No, I don't.*
A [3]*I hear you work for / Is this your first time* at the congress?
B No, I was here last year. [4]*What do you think of it? / Please take a seat.*
A It's really interesting and nice to meet new people.

2 Each phrase in *italics* has an extra word. ~~Cross it out.~~

A Hi, I'm Mia Pieczek from Slovakia. [1]*I hear you do work for Motorola.*
B [2]*Yes, that's is right.*
A You're my customer in Slovakia! [3]*Would you like get another coffee?*
B [4]*No, you're thanks.* I'm fine.
A OK. Well, I'd like one, so I'll [5]*see me you later.*
B Yes. [6]*Nice to talking to you.*

3 Put the words in the right order

1 join / can / you / I
________?
2 you / hear / I / for / KPMG / work
________.
3 something / get / can / you / I
________?
4 you / think / exhibition / what / of / the / do
________?
5 me / please / excuse
________.

Past simple: irregular verbs

Many verbs are irregular and don't take *-ed* in the past simple.

go → went

come → came

have → had

take → took

For a list of irregular verbs and their past simple forms, see page 102.

For how to form sentences and questions in the past simple, see Practice file 5 on page 87.

Time expressions

Use time expressions to say **when** something happened in the past.

last night	*four years ago*
last Tuesday	*in 2008*
last week	*on 26th January*
yesterday	*when I was in Japan*
two days ago	

Time expressions are usually at the end of the sentence.

*I left my job **in 2007**.*
*I flew to Milan **yesterday**.*
*We didn't finish the report **last week**.*

Time expressions can go at the beginning of the sentences to give them more importance.

***Yesterday** I was so busy, I didn't have a break.*

1 Match verbs 1–10 to their past simple forms a–j.

1 do ___	a went
2 take ___	b took
3 give ___	c met
4 spend ___	d left
5 meet ___	e gave
6 go ___	f had
7 fly ___	g spent
8 have ___	h did
9 leave ___	i saw
10 see ___	j flew

2 Complete this email using the past simple form of the verb in brackets.

Subject: Trip to Hawaii - I'm back!

Hi Timo,

I'm back from the trip. It was great. We [1] ________ (fly) with United Airlines in Business Class! Julio [2] ________ (meet) us at the airport when we arrived. We [3] ________ (spend) two weeks visiting customers which was very interesting. Then we [4] ________ (have) a short holiday and [5] ________ (do) some sightseeing. We [6] ________ (not see) Heike unfortunately – we [7] ________ (leave) before she [8] ________ (come) back from her holiday. Anyway, can you tell me what happened in the company in the last three weeks?

Thanks,

Clio

3 Look at this diary. Complete the sentences using the past simple and the time expressions in the list. Today is the 11th.

last Thursday   yesterday   last night
a week ago   two days ago

MON 2	TUES 3	WEDS 4	THURS 5	FRI 6
		Go to Warsaw	Give presentation to the Board	

MON 9	TUES 10	WEDS 11	THURS 12	FRI 13
Leave Warsaw	Meet Jakob for lunch 8 p.m. see the new Bond film			

1 I ________ to Warsaw ________.
2 I ________ a presentation to the Board ________.
3 I ________ Warsaw ________.
4 I ________ Jakob for lunch ________.
5 I ________ the new Bond film ________.

Working with words

1 Complete this text with the best option from a, b, or c below.

This is my department. We [1]__________ customer orders. Ahmed [2]__________ the team and he [3]__________ which customers we work with. Sometimes, he [4]__________ problems with the customers' orders too. I [5]__________ the financial side: invoices and payment. I [6]__________ the invoices are correct and [7]__________ payment agreements to suit our different customers. We [8]__________ the Logistics department – they inform us when the orders are delivered.

	a	b	c
1	**a** develop	**b** are responsible for	**c** plan
2	**a** is in charge of	**b** plans	**c** checks
3	**a** manages	**b** plans	**c** develops
4	**a** controls	**b** is in charge of	**c** deals with
5	**a** check	**b** plan	**c** manage
6	**a** am responsible for	**b** deal with	**c** check
7	**a** develop	**b** control	**c** plan
8	**a** are in charge of	**b** work with	**c** check

2 Complete this crossword with the names of departments.

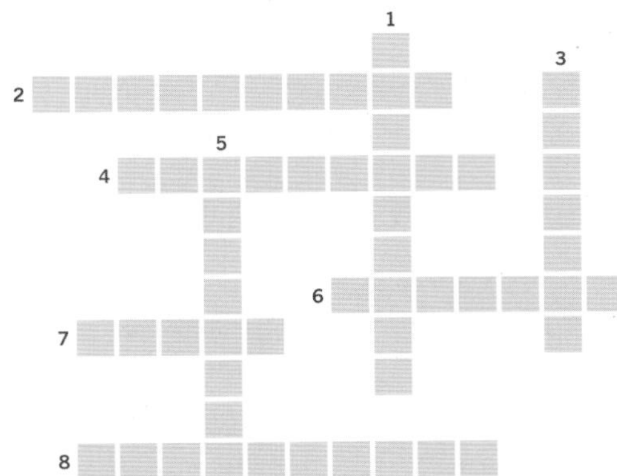

1 is responsible for deliveries
2 is in charge of making the products
3 deals with questions and problems from customers: Customer __________
4 plans advertising for the company
5 plans and develops new products: __________ and Development
6 is in charge of the money in the company
7 deals with the employees in the company: __________ Resources
8 manages the computer network: Information __________

Business communication

1 Put this conversation in the right order.

a ___ And this is your visitor's pass.
b ___ OK. Can you sign here, please?
c ___ OK, thanks.
d ___ Thanks.
e ___ Please take a seat. Mrs Hayek will be right down.
f ___ Yes, certainly.
g ___ My name's Roland Perry. I have an appointment with Mrs Hayek at 10 o'clock.

2 Put the words in *italics* in the right order.

A Mr Perry?
B Yes, hello, you must be Mrs Hayek.
A That's right, *meet / nice / to / you*
[1]______________________________.
B And you.
A *OK / you / us / Did / find*
[2]______________________________?
B It was no problem, your directions were very clear.
A *Would / coffee / like / you / a*
[3]______________________________?
B No, I'm fine thanks.
A OK, well *let / show / me / round / you*
[4]______________________________.
This is our main building …

3 Complete the conversation with these phrases.

have an appointment with	Nice to see you again
Would you like a coffee	will be right with you
let me introduce you to	Can you sign here, please

A Good morning I [1]____________________ Jeff Bernstein.
B [2]______________________________?
A Sure.
B Take a seat. Mr Bernstein [3]____________________.
…
A Jeff! [4]______________________________.
C Yes, you too. [5]__________________________?
A Yes, please. Milk, no sugar.
C Oh, [6]____________________ Alex, my PA. He's in charge of the admin and our team.

Language at work | Prepositions of place and movement

Prepositions of place

To describe the position of something or someone.

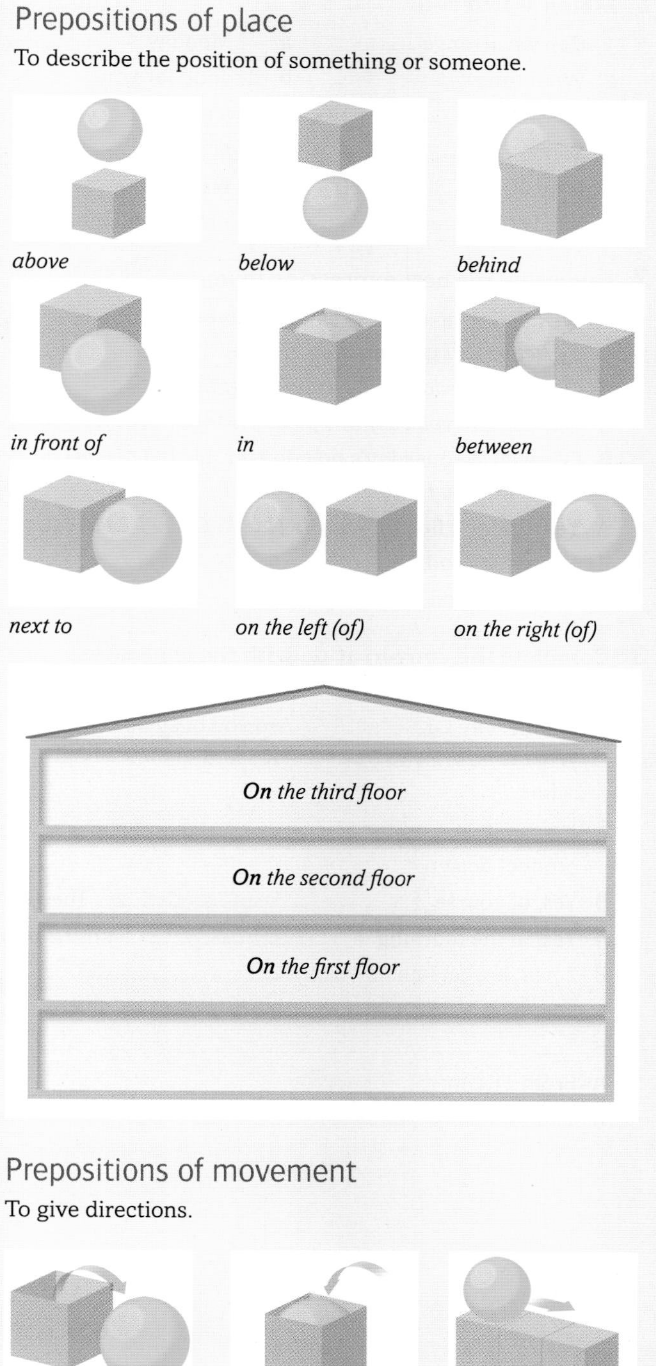

Prepositions of movement

To give directions.

out of *into* *along*

past *up* *down*

1 You are on the stairs. Look at this plan and complete the sentences with words from the list.

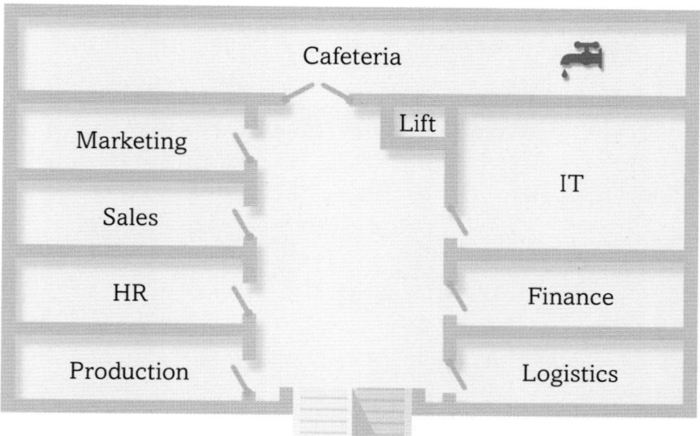

on the right	on the left	behind	on
in	next to	between	in front of

1. Production is ____________ HR.
2. Finance is ____________ Logistics and IT.
3. You are ____________ the first floor.
4. The water fountain is ____________ the cafeteria.
5. Logistics is ____________.
6. Marketing is the last door ____________.
7. The lift is ____________ the cafeteria.
8. Marketing is ____________ Sales.

2 Read these directions and look at the plan in 1. Where do the directions take you?

1. Start at the stairs. Go past HR and then turn left. ____________
2. Go left out of IT and along the corridor. They are in front of you. ____________
3. Go out of the cafeteria, turn right, and go into the room. ____________
4. Go into the lift and up one floor. ____________

3 Correct the mistakes in *italics*.

Business Tower. JEB Electronics. Our offices:
We are *in* [1]________ the 15th floor. Lifts are *in front* [2]________ Reception. Take the lift to the 15th floor and turn left – *in* [3]________ the right is a coffee area. *Next* [4]________ the coffee area is a meeting room. Go *along* [5]________ the meeting room on your right. We are *between of* [6]________ the meeting room and the stairs. Finance and HR are *below* [7]________ on the 16th floor.
Car parking is underground – *above* [8]________ the offices. Ask for a pass at the security desk *on right* [9]________ before you drive in.

Working with words

1 Complete these sentences and use the answers to complete the crossword.

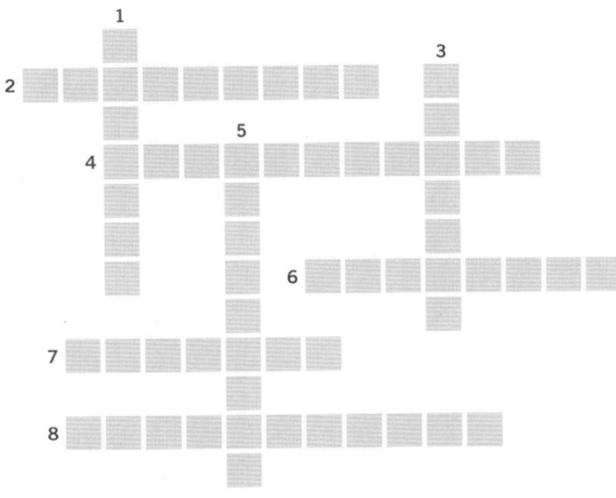

1 As a doctor, I must be ________ about the medicines I give to my patients.
2 My project manager often has problems to deal with, but she is very ________, and usually solves them.
3 I spend a lot of time looking at numbers and budgets. It's not always easy to stay ________.
4 When I started in my company six years ago, I wasn't very ________, but now I know all about the job.
5 In my job, you have to think quickly and be really ________.
6 It is important to stay ________ with the customers.
7 People don't always understand about IT, so I have to be ________ when I try to explain how things work.
8 When we interview for new advertising executives, we look for people who are ________.

2 Complete the conversation with these phrases.

isn't very good
a qualification in
doesn't have any experience in
good at
has a lot of experience in

A We're looking for an advertising assistant and we have a strong candidate. She has [1]________ marketing. She is imaginative and energetic, but she [2]________ our product range.
B I don't think that's a problem – she can learn that. She's [3]________ organizing and planning, I saw some of her work at the interview. She also [4]________ managing people.
A Yes, but she [5]________ at presenting – she was terrible at the interview.
B She can do a presentation course to help her though.

Business communication

1 Match 1–6 to a–f.

1 Can we arrange ___
2 What time ___
3 I'm free on ___
4 Sorry, ___
5 Is 10.00 ___
6 Are you free ___

a … Monday.
b … good for you?
c … a meeting?
d … at lunchtime?
e … are you free?
f … I'm busy then.

2 Underline the best expression in *italics*.

A We need to discuss the sales conference. [1]*Can we arrange a meeting? / I can't meet on Tuesday.*
B OK, [2]*is Thursday OK? / I can't meet then.*
A Oh, no, [3]*are you busy at 5 p.m.? / sorry, I'm busy then.*
B OK, well Wednesday's no good for me, but [4]*I can't meet then / are you free on Friday?*
A Yes. Friday's fine for me. [5]*Is 11 a.m. OK? / 12.00 is good.*
B 11 a.m. is good.
A Great. See you on Friday, then.

3 Complete the conversation with these phrases.

can't meet
Wednesday OK
What time are you free
is fine
Wednesday's good
Are you busy on
We need to meet about

A [1]________ the problem with the product design.
B Yes, of course. [2]________ Tuesday?
A Yes, in the morning. I [3]________ until 2 p.m.
B 2 p.m. is a bit late. Is [4]________?
A Yes, [5]________.
B [6]________?
A From 11 a.m.
B 11 a.m. [7]________ for me.

Present continuous

Form

Positive: Subject + *am / is / are* + *-ing*

*I **am** / **'m** **writing** the monthly report.*
*He **is** / **'s** **working** from home.*
*They **are** / **'re** **meeting** the MD.*

Negative: Subject + *am / is / are not* + *-ing*

*I **am not** / **'m not** **working** at home today.*
*She **is not** / **isn't** **having** her lunch.*
*You **are not** / **aren't** **talking** to Security.*

Questions: (Question word) + *am / is / are* + subject + *-ing*?

***Am** I **working** with the new customer today?*
***Is** it **raining** today?*
***Are** we **looking** at the right report?*

Short answers: Don't repeat the main verb.

*A Am I working with the new customer today? B Yes, you **are**.*
*A Are we looking at the right report? B No, we **aren't**.*

Spelling

Most verbs: add *-ing* to the verb

*study → **studying** / start → **starting***

Verbs ending with *-e*: replace *-e* with *-ing*

*arrive → **arriving***

Verbs ending with vowel + consonant: double the last consonant and add *-ing*

*stop → **stopping***

Use

To describe a temporary or changing situation.

***Are** you **working** on any interesting new projects?*

To describe an action happening at the moment of speaking.

*A What **are** you **doing**?*
*B We**'re interviewing** someone for the new job.*

To describe current trends.

*We **are employing** more people in the IT sector.*

1 Complete this email using the present continuous of the verbs in brackets.

Subject: new position questions / update

Hi Max,
Here's some information about the new position:
Talvinder can't take the new job because she [1]__________ (finish) her university studies. We [2]__________ (contact) some of the other applicants from the interviews last week.
Janis [3]__________ (check) their qualifications again and I [4]__________ (arrange) second interviews. We [5]__________ (not invite) applicants from abroad – this takes too long.
I need some help from you with the interviews – do you have time or [6]__________ (you plan) the HR conference at the moment? Please let me know.
Regards
F

2 Read the dialogue and answer questions a and b.

1 A Are you coming to the meeting now?
2 B No, sorry. I'm working on this presentation.
3 A But Abi is here from South Africa – he's only staying three days.
4 B I know, but Konrad is waiting for it. Anyway, what's Abi's news?
5 A Well, he isn't managing the sales team any more.
6 B What's he doing now, then?
7 A He's helping set up a new sales office in Cape Town.

a Which lines are about a temporary or changing situation? __________

b Which lines are about something happening at the time of speaking? __________

3 Correct the mistakes.

1 Where Zoran and Judith going?
____

2 They're do a course on presentations at the InterContinental today.
____

3 Are you comming to the meeting?
____

4 He not leading the sales team.
____

5 We training to become software engineers.
____

6 Are they meet at the Dorchester?
____

Working with words

1 Complete this email with words from the list.

up-to-date fast wide low friendly high

Our [1]________ range of products is of [2]________ quality and we always offer [3]________ prices. We produce our products using modern machines and [4]________ technology. You can see all the products in our brochure and read about our [5]________ delivery times and [6]________ customer service.

Please call us or order online.

2 Choose the correct adjective from a, b, or c.

1 We use ___ technology to build our systems.
2 Don't buy from BNS, their prices are too ___.
3 We have a ___ choice of products.
4 Our new offices are in a ___ location.
5 We offer a ___ delivery time for urgent orders.
6 They are expensive, but they produce ___-quality products.

1	**a** friendly	**b** low	**c** up-to-date
2	**a** high	**b** fast	**c** bad
3	**a** up-to-date	**b** wide	**c** high
4	**a** slow	**b** good	**c** wide
5	**a** fast	**b** expensive	**c** good
6	**a** wide	**b** bad	**c** high

3 Put the letters in *italics* in the right order to complete the presentation.

We are very competitive and are number two in the market. Why? We offer *findlrey* [1]________ customer service. We can guarantee fast *dylvreei tmie* [2]________ of our products and, although they are sometimes *epxnseiev* [3]________, the products are high *qyultai* [4]________ and there is a wide *coihce* [5]________. The customer service office is also in a *odog* [6]________ location for our customers.

Business communication

1 Underline the correct word in *italics*.

A I have two quotes here for office printers. It's difficult to choose one.
B How do they [1]*compare / better*?
A Lexi is [2]*difference / similar* to Samsonic.
B So what's the [3]*difference / compare*?
A The [4]*advantage / better* of the Lexi is it works with a wireless network.
B That sounds good.
A Yes, but it's more expensive.
B The Samsonic is cheaper, but the [5]*comparison / disadvantage* is it is more difficult to use and isn't wireless.
A I [6]*choice / prefer* the Lexi – it's a higher price but better for our office.
B OK.

2 Put this conversation in the right order. The first and last lines are correct.

a _1_ **A** I have two hotels that look good. Which should we book?
b ___ **B** Let's choose Mercure – breakfast is included, we have transport, and we can get a taxi to the centre of town.
c ___ **A** Well, Mercure is similar to Ibis. Mercure has breakfast included, but Ibis doesn't.
d ___ **B** How do they compare?
e ___ **A** Exactly. But the disadvantage of Ibis is it only has a suite free – no single rooms.
f ___ **B** So we don't need a hire car?
g ___ **A** Yes, breakfast is good, but the advantage of Ibis is its location. It's more central.
h ___ **B** Well I'd like breakfast in the price.
i ___ **B** Oh, does Mercure have single rooms?
j ___ **A** Yes, and the advantage of Mercure is we can have free pick up from the airport.
k _11_ **A** OK – I'll book it.

Language at work | Comparatives

Comparatives

Form

One-syllable adjectives (also some two-syllable adjectives)

Adjectives ending in a consonant: add *-er*

fast → *faster*

Adjectives ending in *-e*: add *-r*

wide → *wider*

Adjectives ending in a vowel + consonant: double the consonant and add *-er*

big → *bigger*

Adjectives ending in *-y*: replace the *-y* with *-ier*

easy → *easier*

Long adjectives – 2 syllables or more

Put *more* **before** the adjective. The adjective doesn't change.

difficult → ***more** difficult*

Irregular adjectives

good → *better*
bad → *worse*

Use

Use a comparative form to say how something is different from something else.

I prefer online shopping because it has a wider choice.

Than

To compare two things use *than* after the adjective.

*A Daewoo is **cheaper than** an Audi.*
*Sofitel is **more expensive than** Novotel.*
*Express delivery is **faster than** standard delivery.*

1 Put these adjectives in the correct row in the table and then add their comparative forms.

friendly   expensive   low   experienced
easy   difficult   fast   cheap

Adjective	Comparative
1	+ *-er*
______	______
______	______
______	______
2	+ *-ier*
______	______
______	______
3	+ *more*
______	______
______	______
______	______

2 Correct the mistakes.

1 easyJet is often more cheap than British Airways. ______
2 Vodafone offers a gooder service than my phone provider. ______
3 Our office is in a more expensive location like our competitor's. ______
4 Spanish is easyer to learn than Japanese. ______
5 Our customers are often more experienced that our technicians. ______
6 The competitors offer more lower prices than us. ______
7 The new mobile phone is more difficulter to use than the old model. ______
8 Their customer service is worser than before. ______

3 Complete this text with words from the list.

friendlier   higher   expensive   wider   than
more (x2)   easier   better   worse

REPORT: Our market position in comparison to our competitor in the supermarket business.

- Our products are often [1]______ expensive, but we offer a [2]______ choice [3]______ them.
- Quality of our products is always [4]______ than theirs.
- Their sales staff are well trained and [5]______ experienced than our shop assistants.
- Customers say our staff are [6]______ than the competitor's.
- Our stores are in more [7]______ locations, but we are [8]______ to find than the competitor.

In conclusion, it's not possible to say our store is [9]______ or [10]______ than the competitor. We have different qualities.

10 | Practice file

Working with words

1 Complete this email with words from the list.

decisions ideas solutions
problems in a team meetings

Subject: my new job!

Hi Xander,

My new job's great – I'm so glad I moved departments. In this job we work [1]__________. I'm the assistant to the technicians who find [2]__________ for our customers. I don't make [3]__________ or solve [4]__________, but it's my job to tell the team about changes and new systems. Sometimes I attend [5]__________ where we work together to develop [6]__________ for the future. It makes a nice change to be part of a team.

How's your job?

2 Complete these sentences, then find the words in the word search.

1 I usually __________ a meeting every Tuesday.
2 It was a __________ decision to close the factory.
3 I called the Helpdesk because I had a __________ problem.
4 Our bosses want us to __________ solutions to our customers' problems.
5 We have more ideas when we __________ in a team.
6 At the brainstorming meetings we __________ ideas for marketing campaigns.
7 Lenny had some __________ ideas for the team-building weekend.
8 Roberto must __________ the right decisions so the project doesn't cost more money.
9 We have ten urgent orders and there's a transport strike – we don't know how to __________ the problem.
10 The company doesn't allow Internet surfing – that's HR's __________ decision.

I	G	H	L	F	F	D	L	J	A
H	V	E	U	X	E	I	A	O	U
W	B	E	E	V	W	F	N	H	E
X	Q	K	E	Z	A	F	I	D	Q
U	A	L	Z	E	C	I	F	G	Y
M	O	X	F	E	S	C	D	O	U
P	W	O	R	K	V	U	R	O	H
D	N	E	T	T	A	L	T	D	B
B	V	J	J	U	W	T	O	I	L
N	I	P	T	S	W	U	G	S	Y

Business communication

1 Complete this conversation with phrases from the list.

Do you think I think What do you think
my opinion Yes, I agree

A [1]__________ about our new advertisement?
B [2]__________ it's the best one so far.
A [3]__________.
B [4]__________ the picture is big enough?
A Oh yes, but in [5]__________, the logo should be smaller.

2 Put the words in *italics* in the right order to continue the conversation from 1.

B *I / agree / don't* [1]__________.
The logo is the most important thing. I like the colours of the packaging – *opinion / your / what's* [2]__________?
A *not / I'm / sure / so* [3]__________.
B *I / we / should / think* [4]__________ make the packaging more interesting with the same colours.
A *true / that's* [5]__________.
It's not the most attractive box for such a great product.

3 Underline the best option in *italics*.

1 A What's your opinion?
B *That's true. / Well, I think …*
2 A I think we should change suppliers.
B *What do you think? / I'm not so sure.*
3 A I don't think that's a good idea.
B *I disagree. / In my opinion.*
4 A What do you think?
B *That's true. / In my opinion, …*
5 A In my opinion, it's a waste of time.
B *I think we should. / Yes, I agree.*

4 Write the missing word / letter in these sentences.

1 What you think? __________
2 That true. __________
3 Do think our company is the best? __________
5 I not so sure. __________
6 My opinion, we should stop production. __________

Language at work | Present continuous | Superlatives

Present continuous

Form

See **Practice file 8** for how to form the present continuous.

Use

Present

For an action happening at the time of speaking.
For a temporary situation.
For a current trend.

See **Practice file 8** for more information.

Future

To describe a fixed arrangement in the future. We usually know the time of the arrangement.

The goods are arriving ***this afternoon****.*
I'm going to New York ***next month****.*
He's taking some holiday ***next week****.*

Superlatives

Form

One-syllable adjectives (also some two-syllable adjectives)

Adjectives ending in a consonant: add *-est*

fast → the fastest

Adjectives ending in *-e*: add *-st*

wide → the widest

Adjectives ending in a vowel + consonant: double the consonant and add *-est*

big → the biggest

Adjectives ending in *-y*: replace the *-y* with *-iest*

easy → the easiest

Long adjectives – 2 syllables or more

Put *the most* **before** the adjective. The adjective doesn't change.

difficult → ***the most*** *difficult*

Irregular adjectives

good → the best
bad → the worst

Remember: ***the*** is always used before the superlative.

Use

To compare more than two things.

John's idea was good. Ingrid's idea was better. But, of the three, Ling's idea was ***the best****.*

1 Complete this conversation using the present continuous form of the verbs in the list.

go finish take (x2) visit do
leave meet have work

A Where's Katja? What [1]________ she d________?
B She [2]________ f________ an email.
A But my plane [3]________ l________ in two hours and she [4]________ t________ me to the airport.
B I'll tell her to hurry. [5]________ you v________ our clients when you arrive?
A No, I [6]________ g________ straight to the hotel – we [7]________ m________ in the evening. We [8]________ h________ dinner together.
B [9]________ you t________ the presentation with you?
A Yes, but I [10]________ still w________ on the introduction. I can finish it on the plane.
B Well, have a good flight.
A Thanks, Michi.

2 Are these sentences from 1 talking about the present (*P*) or the future (*F*)?

1 What's she doing? ___
2 She's finishing an email. ___
3 My plane's leaving in two hours. ___
4 She's taking me to the airport. ___
5 Are you visiting our clients when you arrive? ___
6 We're meeting in the evening. ___
7 Are you taking the presentation with you? ___
8 I'm still working on the introduction. ___

3 Tick (✓) the correct sentence.

1 **a** That was the most important decision in my whole career.
  b That was most important decision in my whole career.
2 **a** I think Gina has the goodest marketing idea.
  b I think Gina has the best marketing idea.
3 **a** My mobile phone is the most up-to-date I could find.
  b My mobile phone is the most up-to-datest I could find.
4 **a** Our competitor is the bigest company in the market.
  b Our competitor is the biggest company in the market.
5 **a** That Internet provider is the most expensive, but offers the bestest service.
  b That Internet provider is the most expensive, but offers the best service.
6 **a** The German manufacturer makes the highest quality goods in our field.
  b The German manufacturer makes the most highest quality goods in our field.

Working with words

1 Complete this text with words from the list.

queues terminal check-in
hand luggage business class aisle seat

Customer Notice

Please arrive at the ¹______ building at least 90 minutes before your flight leaves. You are allowed 5 kg of ²______. For ³______ passengers, a special ⁴______ desk is available with no long ⁵______. No seat numbers are allocated, but for an extra charge you can reserve a window or ⁶______ when you book your flight.

2 Complete this dialogue with the vowels (a, e, i, o, and u).

A Everyone says planes are the fastest way to travel, but I disagree. The [1]t__rm__n__ls are always busy and what about the [2]d__l__ys?

B Yes, you're right. You have to wait at [3]ch__ck-__n. And there's another wait at [4]p__ssp__rt c__ntr__l.

A I always go to the [5]b__s__n__ss cl__ss lounge for some free food and drink before I go to the [6]g__t__!

B Well I can't do that – I always travel [7]__c__n__my. But I only take [8]h__nd l__gg__g__ so I don't have to wait when I arrive.

A Yes, so do I. You must be really careful which airline you choose too: some don't help you when the flight's [9]c__nc__ll__d.

B I know, and some charge you extra for your [10]b__gs!

3 Complete this crossword.

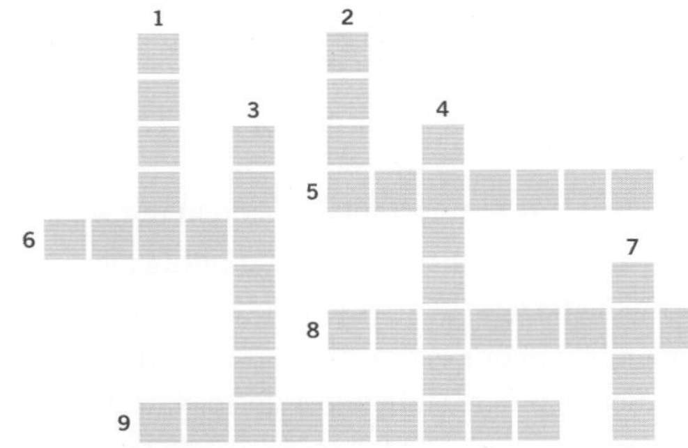

1 a seat in the middle of the plane
2 you wait here before you board the plane
3 you show your ticket here and get your boarding card
4 your passport is checked here: passport ______
5 the cheapest type of ticket
6 a long line you wait in
7 you pack your clothes in these
8 the building at the airport you leave from or arrive at
9 your flight is stopped maybe because of bad weather

Business communication

1 Put this conversation in the right order.

a __ Er ... Oh yes, I have your reservation here. Your room is 503.
b __ Good afternoon, Ms Patel. Is it just for one person?
c __ Thanks.
d __ Good afternoon. I have a reservation for two nights. My name's Patel.
e __ No, that should be fine. We aren't busy on Mondays.
f __ Yes, certainly. Do I need to book a table for dinner tonight?
g __ And can I see your credit card, please?
h __ No, two.

2 Complete these dialogues.

1 **A** D______ y______ h______ a______ v______?
B Sorry, we're fully booked.

2 **A** A double room costs 120 euros a night.
B D______ t______ i______ b______?

3 **A** C______ I b______ a r______?
B Certainly, sir. Can I have your name, please?

4 **A** W______ t______ i______ b______ s______?
B From 6.00 to 9.30.

3 Match 1–5 to a–e to complete the sentences.

1 Could you __
2 Do you __
3 Is there a __
4 Do the rooms have __
5 Can I have __

a ... Internet access?
b ... meeting room?
c ... have room service?
d ... a wake-up call?
e ... order me a taxi?

Language at work | *Going to* | Infinitive of purpose

Going to

Form

Positive: Subject + *am / is / are* + *going to* + verb

I ***am / 'm going to*** *visit the new customer.*
He ***is / 's going to*** *write the next presentation.*
They ***are / 're going to*** *work in Brazil.*

Negative: Subject + *am / is / are not* + *going to* + verb

I ***am not / 'm not going to*** *take the job.*
She ***is not / isn't going to*** *leave the company.*
We ***are not / aren't going to*** *have a meeting about this.*

Questions: (Question word) + *am / is / are* + subject + *going to* + verb

Am I going to *come to the meeting?*
Why is he going to *talk to management?*
Are you going to *visit the suppliers?*

Short answers: Don't repeat *going to*

A *Is he going to talk to management?* ***B*** *No, he* ***isn't****.*
A *Are you going to visit the suppliers?* ***B*** *Yes, I* ***am****.*

Use

To talk about a general plan for a future action or event. It is used to mean the same as *I am planning to …* . There is not necessarily a fixed time in the plan.

I'm ***going to visit*** *Toronto.*
We ***aren't going to eat*** *out in the evening.*
Are you going to take *Friday off?*

Infinitive of purpose

Add an infinitive to say *why* you are doing something.

We're going to meet our suppliers ***to discuss*** *prices.*
They're going to spend a day in New York ***to find*** *a new office.*
I'm going to leave the office at 3 p.m. ***to collect*** *my wife from the airport.*

1 Make sentences from the prompts using *going to*.

1 They / visit / their customers ____________________
2 I / not / ask / Patrice to help ____________________
3 We / take / Tuesday off ____________________
4 It / not / rain today ____________________
5 you / discuss / the contract at the meeting? ____________________
6 I / see / José at the conference ____________________

2 Match 1–6 to a–f to complete the sentences.

1 Franz is going to meet us at the airport before we leave ___
2 We're going to arrive early at check-in ___
3 Samir is going to come to the airport ___
4 Jake is going to attend the conference ___
5 We're going to work late ___
6 I'm going to contact our suppliers ___

a … to find some new customers.
b … to take us to our hotel.
c … to miss the queues.
d … to give us our visas.
e … to ask about the order.
f … to finish the presentation.

3 Correct the mistakes.

1 The airline is going cancel its flights. ____________________
2 Silvia going to attend the meeting instead of me. ____________________
3 Marco are going to confirm his flight details tomorrow. ____________________
4 I'm going to not finish the report by tomorrow. ____________________
5 Are you visit Jess while you're in New York? ____________________
6 Timo's going to call the suppliers for to cancel the order. ____________________
7 Are you going to hold a meeting to discussing the IT problems? ____________________
8 Franz isn't going take the new job. ____________________

Working with words

1 ~~Cross out~~ **the word that *doesn't* match with the noun.**

1	tight / busy / public	schedule
2	busy / annual / quiet	period
3	public / time / annual	holiday
4	tight / busy	deadline
5	annual / time	off
6	public / annual	leave

2 Klaus works for Pioneering, a seed company. He's talking about his job. Replace the phrases in bold in the text with the expressions in the list.

annual leave	deadline	long weekend
public holiday	some time off	busy period

We have a **lot of work** 1__________ at the beginning of the year. The shops need the seeds in February and our **final date** 2__________ to get the seeds ready is the end of January. It doesn't give us much time. I try to take **a break** 3__________ at Easter, and in May we have a **national day off** 4__________, so I usually take a **holiday from Friday to Monday** 5__________. In the summer the company closes for two weeks and we all have our **holidays** 6__________.

3 Complete this email with words from the list.

timetable	annual conference	busy schedules
quiet period	tight	reminder

Subject: Next week

Dear Julio

Thanks for the 1__________ about my presentation at next week's 2__________. Unfortunately, my 3__________ now looks very busy with the preparation for my presentation, and I am worried about the 4__________ deadline for the sales report. I know we all have 5__________ at the moment, but I wanted to ask if I could give you the report a week late. The week after next is going to be a 6__________ for me, so I will have time to do it.

Thanks

Paulo

Business communication

1 Put the words in *italics* in the right order.

A We have a few problems. *The / that / is / situation* 1__________ the ordering system has crashed.

B OK, we have a back-up and the technicians are working to fix it. *The / to / is / aim* 2__________ be working by lunchtime.

A Well, we need to hurry.

B Why? *What / deadline / 's / the* 3__________?

A The courier arrives at 1 p.m. to collect the goods, so *why / we / don't* 4__________ finish the orders we're working on? New orders will have to wait. I'll put a notice on the website to inform customers.

B Good idea. *So / summarize / to* 5__________, the current orders are OK, but new orders aren't. Is that right?

2 Complete this dialogue with phrases from the list.

How much time do we need for	Let's
I'm going to	We've already

A 1__________ spent two days on the presentation and the meeting is tomorrow.

B 2__________ the graphs and figures?

A Well, I'm waiting for Alexi to send them to me.

B 3__________ call him and give him a deadline.

A OK. Can you do that?

B Sure, so you're going to finish as much as you can and 4__________ call Alexi. OK?

3 Complete the phrases and find the hidden word.

1 The _ _ _ _ [_] _ _ _ is two weeks behind.
2 What _ _ _ [_] is the meeting?
3 The [_] _ _ is to sign the contract by March.
4 Why [_] _ _ _ we call the customer?
5 We _ [_] _ _ to finish on Friday.
6 The _ [_] _ _ _ _ _ _ _ is that the goods are late.
7 How long do we [_] _ _ _ for the delivery?
8 Is _ _ [_] _ _ _ _ _ happy with that date?
9 So, to [_] _ _ _ _ _ _ _ _, we call John and …

Present perfect

Form

Positive: Subject + *have / has* + past participle*

*I **have ordered** some more office paper.*
*He **has sent** the invoice to the wrong person.*

Negative: Subject + *have / has not* + past participle*

*We **have not received** your payment.*
*She **hasn't been** to Nepal.*

Questions: (Question word) + *have / has* + subject + past participle*

***Have you contacted** the suppliers?*
*Why **has he gone** to Canada?*

Short answers: Don't repeat the past participle*

A Have you contacted the suppliers?
*B Yes, I **have**.*

*** past participle**

For regular verbs, add *-ed* to the verb, as for the rules for forming the past simple (see Practice file 5 on page 87).

For a list of irregular verbs and their past participles, see page 102.

Use

To talk about an action in the past that has an effect on the present.

I have finished the report and given it to my boss.

Action in the past = finish the report, give it to my boss

Effect on the present = the report is on my boss's desk

Never use the present perfect to talk about an event in the past with a time expression (see Practice file 6 on page 89 for time expressions).

1 **Read this list of tasks then complete the email, saying what you have (✓) and haven't (✗) done.**

Finish the report for Ajax. ✓
Call our suppliers. ✗
Finalize the menu for the buffet reception. ✓
Book hotel rooms for our Thai guests. ✓
Send the timetable of the visit to the guests. ✗
Check Irena's emails. ✓
Cancel Irena's flight to Sweden. ✗

Dear Irena
I have been very busy, so I haven't done everything you asked.
I 1_____________ the report for Ajax.
I 2_____________ our suppliers.
I 3_____________ the menu for the buffet reception.
I 4_____________ hotel rooms for our Thai guests.
I 5_____________ the timetable of the visit to the guests.
I 6_____________ your emails.
I 7_____________ your flight to Sweden.
Regards

2 **Complete this dialogue with the present perfect form of the verb in brackets.**

A 1_____________ (you / send) the order yet?
B No, I 2_____________ (have / not).
A Why not? I 3_____________ (post) them the invoice already!
B The order's not ready. The Production department 4_____________ (have) some problems.
A Oh, I 5_____________ (not / speak) to Jeff from Production today, so no one told me.
B The packing machine 6_____________ (break down) and they 7_____________ (not / fix) it yet.
A OK, I'll call the customers and explain.

3 **Correct the mistakes.**

1 They haven't the order completed. _____________
2 A Have you done the holiday timetable yet?
B Yes, I done. _____________
3 Mikhail haven't replied yet. _____________
4 A Do they have confirmed the hotel booking?
B No, they haven't. _____________
5 I've work in IT development and on the helpdesk. _____________
6 Thiery's took the last car from our car pool. _____________

Irregular verb list

Verb	Past simple	Past participle
be	was / were	been
become	became	become
begin	began	begun
break	broke	broken
bring	brought	brought
build	built	built
burn	burnt / burned	burnt / burned
buy	bought	bought
catch	caught	caught
choose	chose	chosen
come	came	come
cost	cost	cost
cut	cut	cut
deal	dealt	dealt
do	did	done
drink	drank	drunk
drive	drove	driven
eat	ate	eaten
fall	fell	fallen
feed	fed	fed
feel	felt	felt
fight	fought	fought
find	found	found
fly	flew	flown
forget	forgot	forgotten
get	got	got
give	gave	given
go	went	gone / been
grow	grew	grown
have	had	had
hear	heard	heard
keep	kept	kept
know	knew	known
lead	led	led
learn	learnt / learned	learnt / learned
leave	left	left
let	let	let
light	lit	lit

Verb	Past simple	Past participle
lose	lost	lost
make	made	made
meet	met	met
pay	paid	paid
put	put	put
read	read	read
ring	rang	rung
run	ran	run
say	said	said
see	saw	seen
sell	sold	sold
send	sent	sent
set	set	set
show	showed	shown
shut	shut	shut
sing	sang	sung
sit	sat	sat
sleep	slept	slept
speak	spoke	spoken
spell	spelt / spelled	spelt / spelled
spend	spent	spent
stand	stood	stood
steal	stole	stolen
swim	swam	swum
take	took	taken
teach	taught	taught
tell	told	told
think	thought	thought
understand	understood	understood
wear	wore	worn
win	won	won
write	wrote	written

File 01 | Unit 1

Language at work, Exercise 9, page 9

Student A

Ask and answer questions about the people on this site. Write the missing information. Use these questions.

Who is / are …? Is / Are …? What is his / her / their …?
Where is / are … from?

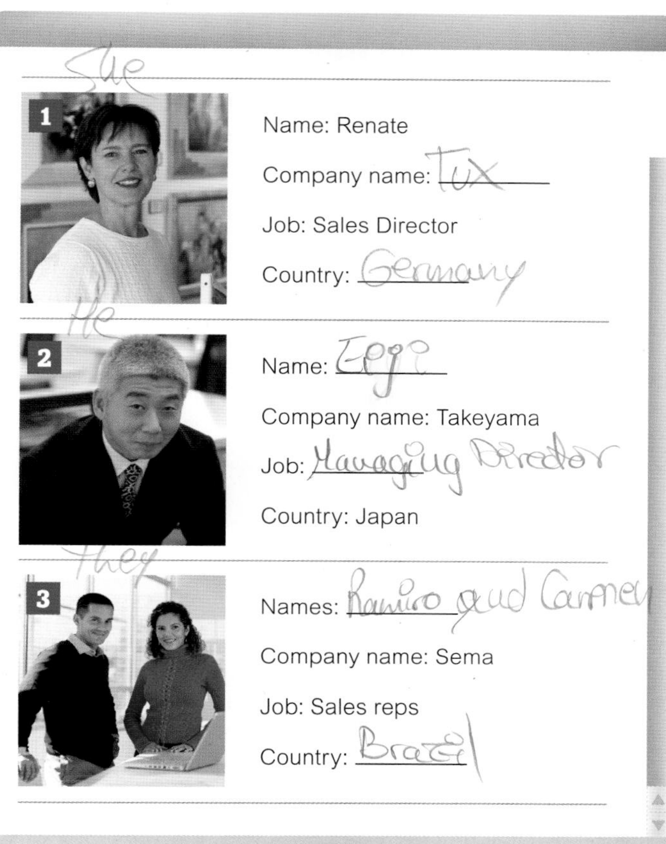

1
Name: Renate
Company name:
Job: Sales Director
Country:
2
Name:
Company name: Takeyama
Job:
Country: Japan
3
Names:
Company name: Sema
Job: Sales reps
Country:

File 02 | Unit 2

Case study, Task, Exercise 3, page 17

Student A

Call Viking. You

- want to place an order
- are interested in a desk (Reference 05GH4).

Ask

- Can I order it by phone?
- Do I get a special price?

File 03 | Unit 3

Working with words, Exercise 8, page 19

Use this information about the pharmaceutical company, Astra Zeneca, for your presentation.

Head office
London, UK

Research and Development
Södertälje, Sweden

Other Research and Development centres
on three continents (Europe, North America, India)

Factories
27 in 19 countries

Sales offices
on five continents:
32 in Europe
16 in North America
12 in Latin America
28 in Asia and the Middle East
13 in Africa, Australia, and New Zealand

File 04 | Unit 3

Business communication, Exercise 3, page 22

Student A

1 Telephone your partner and check these details.

Ms Bebiyon	Tel. 07 364 330?
Mr Gibuvo	Tel. 0034 711 5400?

2 Your partner calls to check these details. Correct any mistakes.

Mr Kassabygy	Tel. 0041 909 5520
Ms Herrera	Tel. 0709 553 627

File 05 | Unit 2

Business communication, Exercise 7, page 16

Student A

1 You want to book rooms at a hotel for a group of six. Telephone the customer service representative (Student B). Ask about the following.
- rooms for next month
- price per room
- special prices for groups

Book the rooms and give your name. Ask for the hotel email address.

2 You are the customer service representative at a hotel. A customer (Student B) wants to book a room for a meeting. Use this information and respond to his / her questions.
- You have a room for next week.
- You can organize lunch and drinks.
- Price: Room = 30 dollars per hour. Lunch = 45 dollars per person.
- No special prices. Price is per hour. For example, 210 dollars for seven hours.

Take the booking and ask the caller to confirm the booking by email. Your email address is conferencehotels@aol.com.

File 06 | Unit 3

Language at work, Exercise 6, page 21

Student A

You are the customer service representative at this hotel. Give Student B information.

Example: *B Is there a bus to the airport?*
A Yes, there's a bus every 30 minutes and there are also buses to the city centre.

The Arabian Garden Hotel

- Bus to airport every 30 minutes and to city centre every 15 minutes.
- No car park, but guests can park on the street. There is also car hire at Reception.
- Two restaurants and one bar.
- Swimming pool, gym, and sauna.
- Internet access in all rooms.
- Conference room for 80 people and four meeting rooms.
- The hotel has a tourist information service and there are day trips to places of interest.

File 07 | Unit 3

Business communication, Exercise 6, page 22

Student A

Call 1

You are Megumi Yoshida. Telephone Michelle McGoldrick about your hotel reservation. You want the hotel details as soon as possible. Your phone number is 078 546 2394.

Call 2

You are Youssuf Hussein's assistant. He is at lunch. Answer the phone and take a message.

Message for: ....

From: ....

Phone number: ....

Calling about: ....

....

Please call back: ☐ Urgent: ☐

File 08 | Unit 3

Case study, Task, Exercise 1, page 23

Student A

	A	B	C
Location	business park of a big city		
Other businesses near	4 banks, offices, college, 2 restaurants		
Transport	tram / underground		
Type of customers	office workers, students		
Parking	difficult		

File 09 | Unit 5

Working with words, Exercise 8, page 31

Student A

1 You are away on a business trip. Student B has two emails for you and telephones you for help. Ask what the emails are about and give the following instructions.
- Email 1: Reply and attach electronic copy. It's in the folder marked 'Newbroch'.
- Email 2: Forward it to HR and reply to the applicant.

2 Student B is on a training course. You check his or her email. Telephone B and explain the emails. Ask what to do. Make notes and check you understand.

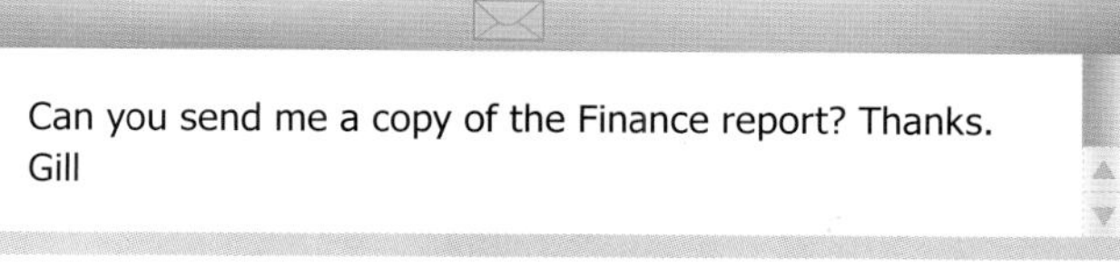

Can you send me a copy of the Finance report? Thanks.
Gill

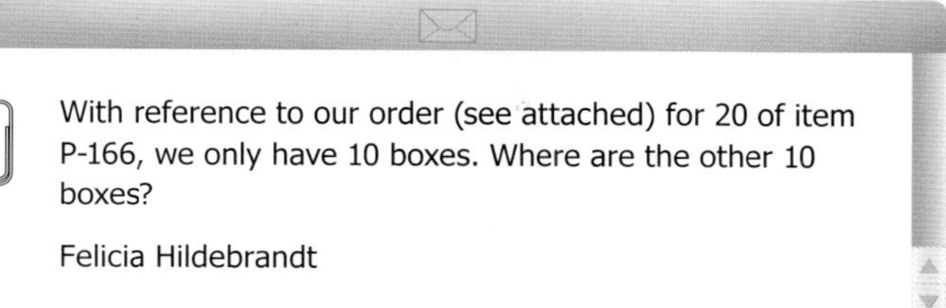

With reference to our order (see attached) for 20 of item P-166, we only have 10 boxes. Where are the other 10 boxes?

Felicia Hildebrandt

File 10 | Unit 4

Business communication, Exercise 5, page 28

Student A

Role-play these situations.

1 You have a heavy box to carry to your office. Student B speaks to you.
2 Student B asks you for help. Respond.
3 Student B looks sick. Offer help.
4 You need to do 50 photocopies for a meeting starting now. Ask Student B for help.

File 11 | Unit 5

Language at work, Exercise 11, page 33

Student A

1 You received this telephone message. Ask your partner for the missing information. Use the question words in brackets.

Mr Simons called at ________ a.m. (When ...?)
He called about ________. (What ...?)
He didn't come to the meeting because ________. (Why ...?)
He wanted to know ________ of the next conference. (What ...?)
Please call him back if you want him to speak at the conference.

2 Now answer your partner's questions about the information in this telephone message.

From: Mr Koch
Time: 2.00 p.m.
Subject: Trip to Germany last week.
Message: Hans was sick – another meeting next month.

File 12 | Unit 5

Business communication, Exercise 4, page 34

Student A

Read more information about the problems in the email.
- Astrid, the receptionist, is sick today.
- You called IT about the printers, but no one answered.
- You didn't remember to book the tickets.
- You can buy Ellen a leaving present.

Now telephone your partner.

1 Explain and solve the problems together.
2 Promise action.

File 13 | Unit 5

Case study, Task, Exercise 3, page 35

Student A

Call 1

You are the Tasks Everyday assistant.
- Call Balfour Furnishings.
- Explain the problem about Tony.
- Ask your client to go to the meeting at 3.00 p.m.

Call 2

You work for Omega. You receive a phone call.
- Your boss isn't in the office.
- Take a message and promise to call back.

File 14 | Unit 6

Practically speaking, Exercise 2, page 39

Student A

1 Look at these photos and answer your partner's questions about this trip.

2 Now ask your partner these questions about his / her trip.
1 How was the journey?
2 How was the hotel?
3 How was the food?
4 How was the meeting?
5 How was the city?

File 15 | Unit 7

Language at work, Exercise 3, page 44

Student A

1 Describe this company plan to Student B.
Example: *The cafeteria is below Sales and Marketing.*

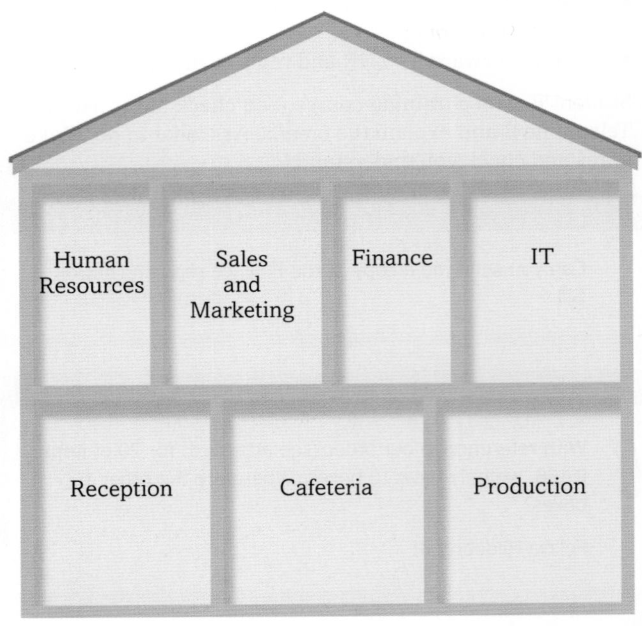

2 Listen to Student B. Write in the rooms and departments.

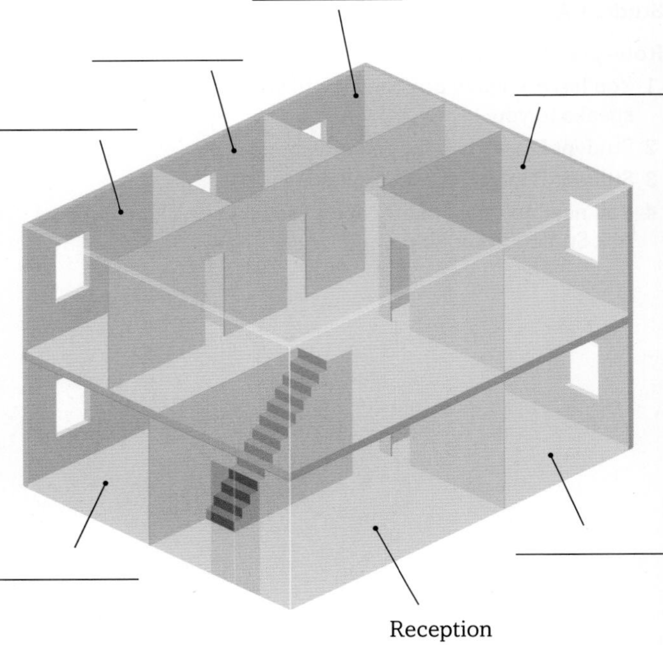

File 16 | Unit 5

Language at work, Exercise 5, page 32

Student A

1 You weren't at a presentation last week. Your partner was. Check if the report below is correct.

Example: ***A*** *Was it on Tuesday morning?*
B *Yes, it was. / No, it wasn't. It was on Thursday morning.*

Presentation: Future Plans
Time: Tuesday morning (?)
Present: Jan, Lydia, Janusz, Carlos (?)
Venue: The conference room (?)
Speaker: Managing Director (?)

2 Now answer your partner's questions about this report.

Presentation: Profits for this year
Time: Wednesday morning
Present: Jan, Lydia, Janusz, Carlos, Piotr
Venue: The conference room
Speaker: Financial Director

File 17 | Unit 8

Business communication, Exercise 6, page 52

Student A

You are Chen. Here's your calendar on Thursday.

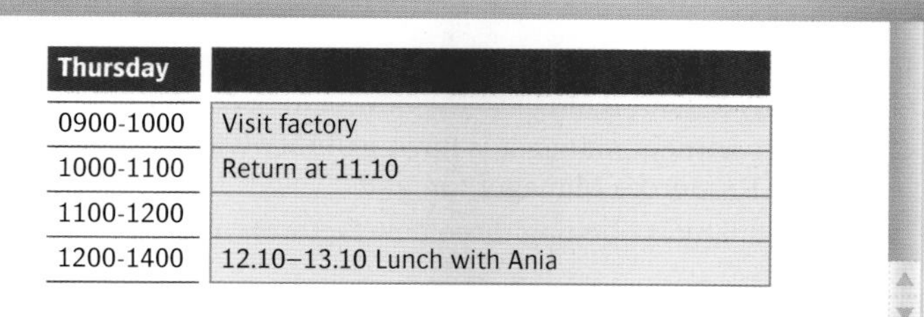

Thursday	
0900-1000	Visit factory
1000-1100	Return at 11.10
1100-1200	
1200-1400	12.10–13.10 Lunch with Ania

File 18 | Unit 6

Business communication, Exercise 7, page 40

Student A

Role-play these situations.

1 It's the first morning of an annual conference. It's your first time at the conference. The first session is in Room 125, but where is it? Student B speaks to you.
2 You are in Reception at your company. A visitor wants to see Sara Olsen who is on the third floor. Speak to him / her.

File 19 | Unit 9

Business communication, Exercise 5, page 58

Student A

You and your partner need to choose a new courier company for important deliveries, and a hotel for some two-day training seminars around the country.

- You have quotes from two courier firms.
- Your partner has quotes from two hotels.
- Take turns to ask and tell each other about the quotes, and then make a choice together.

Company: Speed Merchants
Price: €10 per kilometre
Online tracking: Uses up-to-date satellite technology to find a fast route. You can check your package online.
Location: Centres in over 20 cities.

- very friendly staff on the phone
- no discounts

Company: Go Fast
Price: €9.95 per kilometre
Guaranteed delivery: Money back if late.
Location: Centres in 18 cities.

- staff were slow to answer the phone
- no way to check packages online
- offered free delivery for every ten

File 20 | Unit 8

Activity, Stage 2, page 53

Student A

MONDAY
09.00 doctor
11.00 – 12.00 HR weekly meeting
15.00 – 17.00 meeting with personnel agency

TUESDAY
13.00 – 14.00 lunch – out of office
15.00 – 17.00 team meeting

WEDNESDAY
15.00 – 17.00 meeting with department heads

THURSDAY
14.00 – leave work, take Jamie to dentist

FRIDAY

File 21 | Unit 9

Case study, Task, Exercise 3, page 59

Morrisons is top for quality products, customer service, and values

Morrisons is 'Retailer of the Year' for the second year! Retired owner, Sir Ken Morrison, collected his award in London.

These are the changes they made.

- Different logo to give a newer, more attractive image.
- Employed more qualified staff – butchers, bakers, etc. to prepare fresh food (more than other supermarkets).
- Freshly made food in store – bread, cakes, pizza, etc. (more than other supermarkets).
- Local products – 100% British lamb, pork, etc.
- Wide range of flowers and 'fair-trade' flowers at all prices: to offer more choice for all customers.

File 22 | Unit 10

Language at work, Exercise 11, page 63

There are three candidates for the job of line manager at the Recife factory.

- Look at this information.
- Compare and discuss the three candidates.
- Use the phrases in the list to help you.

... the most experienced ... the most popular
... joined the company earlier than ...
... speaks better Portuguese than ...

2 Who is the best candidate?

MARCIO	PAOLO	LUCY
Factory: Rio	Factory: Recife	Factory: Recife
Work history: Joined the company in 2003 as a line worker.	Work history: Joined the company as line worker last year.	Work history: Joined the company's Denver factory in 2001.
Became team leader for Production line 1 in 2006.	Became team leader for Production line 2 this year.	Became team leader in 2007. Moved to Recife six months ago.
Comments: Very popular with his team. He is looking for jobs in other companies.	Comments: Next month – training course in management skills.	Comments: Her team like her. She is taking Portuguese lessons.

File 23 | Unit 10

Practically speaking, Exercise 3, page 63

Student A

Here is your news. Tell your partner.

1 Everyone in your team likes the new team leader.
2 Your department manager is having dinner with the new Human Resources Manager tonight!
3 The company is opening three new factories abroad.

File 24 | Unit 11

Business communication, Exercise 1, page 70

Student A

61▷ You are Ms Chiang. Listen and write down this information.

- cost of room ____________________
- what it includes ____________________
- check-in time ____________________
- location of hotel ____________________

File 25 | Unit 11

Business communication, Exercise 4, page 70

Student A

1 You need a hotel room. Telephone the Metro Hotel. Ask about
- double rooms and cost for two nights
- breakfast (included?)
- location of hotel.

Your name is: S. Laurukenas
Credit card details:
- American Express
- 9967 4563 1102 3544
- Expiry date: 11/14

2 You are the receptionist at the Excelsior Hotel. Student B telephones to book a room.
- You have double rooms (cost $110 per night).
- Breakfast is extra ($15).
- The hotel is in the centre of the business district.
- Take the caller's name and credit card details.

File 26 | Unit 11

Business communication, Exercise 8, page 70

Student A

Now you are a visitor. Check in and ask for information on the following.

- wake-up call at 6.30 a.m.?
- restaurant in hotel? necessary to book?
- meeting room for tomorrow at 10.00 a.m.?
- sauna and solarium?

File 27 | Unit 11

Case study, Task, Exercise 1, page 71

Student B

You work for Hotel Supreme. Answer the phone call from your partner and give the information.

Hotel name	Hotel Supreme
Location	City centre
Rooms available	30 doubles
Price (including breakfast)	€250
Services	3 meeting rooms 1 conference room All available Offers sightseeing tours in the evening
Restaurant reservation	Only buffet restaurant – can recommend good restaurants nearby
Special group booking rates	No special rates

File 28 | Unit 12

Language at work, Exercise 8, page 75

Student A

Here is a list of your tasks for the week. Ask Student B if he / she has done his / her tasks and say if you have done yours.

Example: ***A*** *Have you ordered a new computer?*
B *Yes, I have.*

You	Done?	Student B
order a new computer	yes	book venue for annual conference?
ship delivery to Argentina	no	write minutes for team meeting?
telephone clients about new product	no	organize meeting with union rep?
email new brochure to clients	yes	ask boss for some time off?

File 29 | Unit 1

Language at work, Exercise 9, page 9

Student B

Ask and answer questions about the people on this site. Write the missing information. Use these questions.

Who is / are ...? Is / Are ...? What is his / her / their ...? Where is / are ... from?

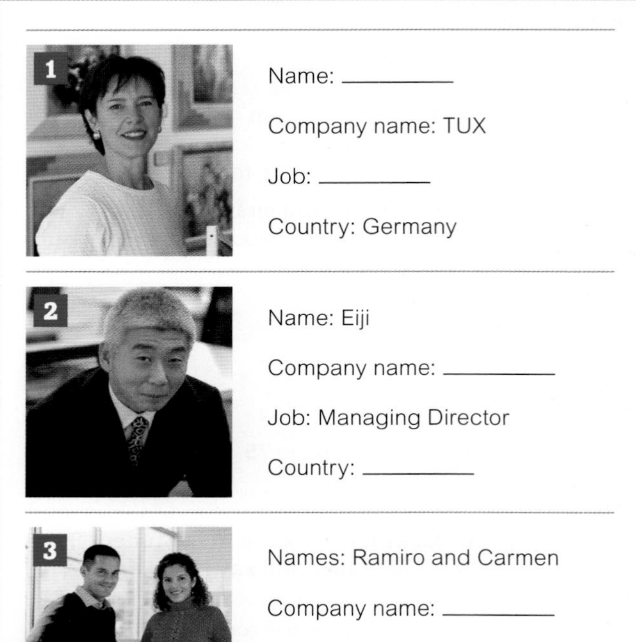

1
Name: ________
Company name: TUX
Job: ________
Country: Germany

2
Name: Eiji
Company name: ________
Job: Managing Director
Country: ________

3
Names: Ramiro and Carmen
Company name: ________
Job: ________
Country: Brazil

File 30 | Unit 2

Case study, Task, Exercise 3, page 17

Student B

You work at Viking. Answer the call and give this information to your customer.

- Yes, you can order by phone and on the Internet.
- No, there's no special price.

Ask for

- customer name
- customer phone number
- customer email address.

File 31 | Unit 2

Business communication, Exercise 7, page 16

Student B

1 You are the customer service representative at a hotel. A customer telephones you (Student A). Use this information and respond to his / her questions.
- You have rooms for next month.
- Prices: double 145 euros, single 115 euros.
- No special prices for groups.

Take the booking and ask the caller to confirm the booking by email. Your email address is expressinns@yahoo.com.

2 You want to book a meeting room for seven hours at a hotel. Telephone the customer service representative (Student A). Ask about the following.
- room for next week
- lunch and drinks
- price
- special price for all day

Book the room and give your name. Ask for the hotel email address.

File 32 | Unit 3

Language at work, Exercise 7, page 21

Student B

You are the customer service representative at this hotel. Give Student A information.

Example: *A Is there a bus to the airport?*
B Yes, there's a bus every 20 minutes.

The Dubai Grand Hotel

- Buses to airport every 20 minutes.
- Car park for 100 guests.
- No restaurant in the hotel. There are some international restaurants near the hotel.
- Swimming pool and gym.
- Internet access in all rooms.
- Bank and post service in hotel.
- Six meeting rooms.
- The hotel has free taxi service to city centre.

File 33 | Unit 12

Business communication, Exercise 4, page 76

Student A

You are in charge of the schedule. You need to schedule the following stages:

- product details and price list
- design
- printing
- sending the brochures to customers

Find out from Students B and C how long each stage takes. You want to send the brochure to clients by 1st November at the latest. Also find out when Students B and C have time off because this will change the schedule.

Discuss the final schedule and write down the stages with all the important dates.

File 34 | Unit 3

Business communication, Exercise 6, page 22

Student B

Call 1

You work in an office with Michelle McGoldrick. She is out. Answer the phone and take a message.

Message for: ....

From: ....

Phone number: ....

Calling about: ....

....

Please call back: ☐ Urgent: ☐

Call 2

You are Henri Watunda. Telephone Youssuf Hussein about your meeting this evening. You are at the Arabian Garden Hotel in Dubai. Your room number is 701. The hotel number is 00971 4228663.

File 35 | Unit 3

Case study, Task, Exercise 1, page 23

Student B

	A	B	C
Location		small town near the sea	
Other businesses near		tourist shops, supermarket	
Transport		walking distance to shops and beach	
Type of customers		lots of tourists, local people, workers	
Parking		yes	

File 36 | Unit 5

Working with words, Exercise 8, page 31

Student B

1 Student A is away on a business trip. You check his or her email. Telephone A and explain the emails. Ask what to do. Make notes and check you understand.

Can I have an order form and a copy of this year's brochure?
Thanks

Jiri
Hanron Solutions

Dear Sir or Madam
Further to your advert for trainee sales person, please find attached a copy of my CV.

2 You are on a training course. Student A checks your email and telephones you for help. Ask what the emails are about and give the following instructions.

- Email 1: It's in a folder called 'Budgets'. Please print her a hard copy.
- Email 2: Forward it to the right department – it's not my responsibility.

File 37 | Unit 3

Business communication, Exercise 3, page 22

Student B

1 Your partner calls to check these details. Correct any mistakes.

Ms Babayan	Tel. 077 364 3300
Mr Jibowo	Tel. 0033 771 5440

2 Telephone your partner and check these details.

Mr Kasebiggy	Tel. 001 908 5220?
Ms Hirrarer	Tel. 070 953 6227?

File 38 | Unit 5

Language at work, Exercise 5, page 32

Student B

1 Your partner wants to know if the report below is correct. You were at the presentation last week. Your partner wasn't. Answer his / her questions.

Example: *A Was it on Tuesday morning?*
B Yes, it was.

Presentation: Future plans
Time: Tuesday morning
Present: Jan, Lydia, Carlos
Venue: Room 305
Speaker: Managing Director

2 Now ask your partner questions about this report.

Presentation: Profits for this year
Time: Thursday morning (?)
Present: Jan, Janusz, Lydia, Carlos (?)
Venue: The conference room (?)
Speaker: Managing Director and Financial Director (?)

File 39 | Unit 5

Language at work, Exercise 11, page 33

Student B

1 Answer your partner's questions about the information in this telephone message.

From: Mr Simons
Time: 9.30 a.m.
Subject: Next month's conference.
Message: In Canada. Date of next conference?

2 You received this telephone message. Ask your partner for the missing information. Use the question words in brackets.

Mr Koch called at ________ p.m. (When ...?)
He called about the ________ last week. (What ...?)
Hans cancelled the meeting because ________. (Why ...?)
We arranged another meeting for ________. (When ...?)
Please call him back.

File 40 | Unit 5

Business communication, Exercise 4, page 34

Student B

Read more information about the problems in the email.

- Your assistant is not very busy today.
- We emailed the wrong invoice. You'll contact them after the meeting.
- The IT department has a training course today and tomorrow.
- You booked a restaurant for Ellen's leaving party.

Your partner telephones you.

1 Explain and solve the problems together.
2 Promise action.

File 41 | Unit 4

Business communication, Exercise 5, page 28

Student B

Role-play these situations.

1 Student A has a heavy box. Offer help.
2 The printer doesn't work. Ask Student A for help.
3 You are sick, but have lots of work to finish. Student A speaks to you.
4 Student A asks you for help. Respond.

File 42 | Unit 5

Case study, Task, Exercise 3, page 35

Student B

Call 1

You are a colleague of Nina at Balfour Furnishings.

- You can't go to the meeting – you have another meeting.
- Promise to call the customer and explain the situation.

Call 2

You are the Tasks Everyday assistant.

- Call Omega.
- Explain the problem with the order form.
- Ask if they want to order the products now over the phone, or send the order form again.

File 43 | Unit 6

Business communication, Exercise 7, page 40

Student B

Role-play these situations.

1 It's the first morning of a conference. You're one of the organizers. Room 125 is on the first floor. You think Student A has a problem. Speak to him / her.
2 You are a visitor at a company. It's your first time at the company. You are here to see Sara Olsen. Student A speaks to you.

File 44 | Unit 8

Business communication, Exercise 5, page 52

Student B

You are Dolores. Here's your calendar on Thursday.

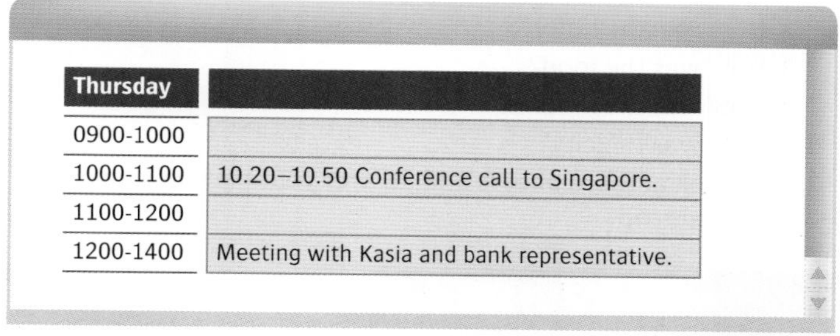

Thursday	
0900-1000	
1000-1100	10.20–10.50 Conference call to Singapore.
1100-1200	
1200-1400	Meeting with Kasia and bank representative.

File 45 | Unit 8

Activity, Stage 2, page 53

Student B

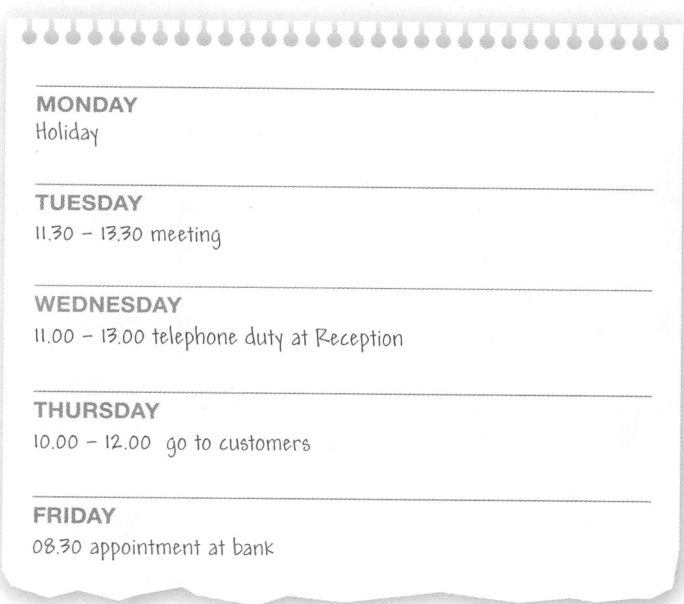

MONDAY
Holiday

TUESDAY
11.30 – 13.30 meeting

WEDNESDAY
11.00 – 13.00 telephone duty at Reception

THURSDAY
10.00 – 12.00 go to customers

FRIDAY
08.30 appointment at bank

File 46 | Unit 6

Practically speaking, Exercise 2, page 39

Student B

1 Ask your partner these questions about his / her trip.
   1 How was the journey?
   2 How was the hotel?
   3 How was the food?
   4 How was the meeting?
   5 How was the city?
2 Now look at these photos and answer your partner's questions about this trip.

File 47 | Unit 7

Language at work, Exercise 3, page 44

Student B

1 Listen to Student A. Write in the rooms and departments.

2 Describe this company plan to Student A.
   Example: *IT is behind Reception.*

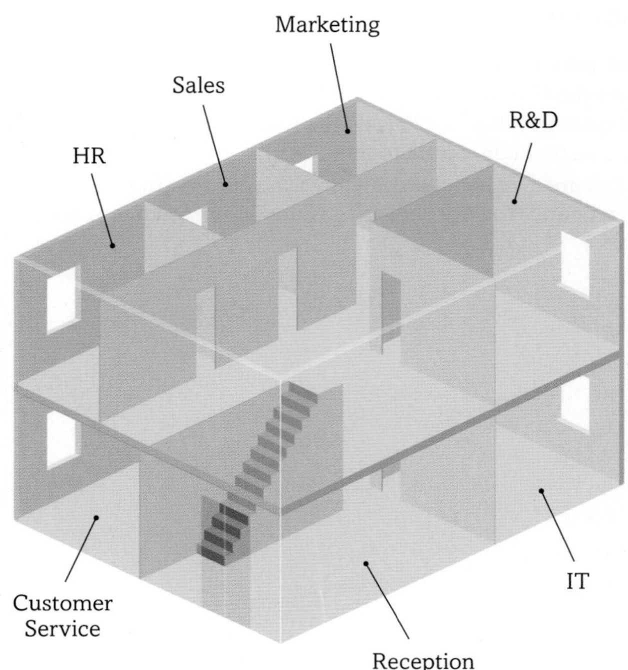

File 48 | Unit 9

Business communication, Exercise 5, page 58

Student B

You and your partner need to choose a new courier company for important deliveries, and a hotel for some two-day training seminars around the country.

- You have quotes from two hotels.
- Your partner has quotes from two courier firms.
- Take turns to ask and tell each other about the quotes, and then make a choice together.

Hotels: InCountry
Price: €5,000 (for ten people)
Facilities: Many hotels provide secretarial service with fax, Internet, printers.
Locations: Over 35 hotels. Hotels are in the countryside, but easy to find.
Leisure: Most hotels have swimming pools and gym facilities.

- all hotels are different and restaurants serve local dishes
- friendly customer service person on the phone

Hotels: Vacationworld
Price: €5,100 (for twelve people)
Facilities: All hotels have two or more meeting rooms.
Locations: 30 hotels near or in city centres.
Leisure: Ten Vacationworld Plus hotels have swimming pools, sauna, and gym.

- staff were polite and helpful
- all hotels are modern; restaurants serve wide range (Italian, Chinese, Indian, etc.)

File 49 | Unit 10

Practically speaking, Exercise 3, page 63

Student B

Here is your news. Tell your partner.

1 Your favourite colleague is leaving the company.
2 Your company won a new contract yesterday.
3 No one's receiving a pay rise this year.

File 50 | Unit 11

Business communication, Exercise 1, page 70

Student B

61▷ You are the hotel receptionist. Listen and write down information about Ms Chiang.

- why she needs a room ______
- how many nights? ______
- credit card details ______

File 51 | Unit 11

Business communication, Exercise 4, page 70

Student B

1 You are the receptionist at the Metro Hotel. Student A telephones to book a room.
   - You have double rooms (cost $150 per night) including breakfast.
   - The hotel is to the right of the central train station.
   - Take the caller's name and credit card details.

2 Now you need a hotel room. Telephone the Excelsior Hotel. Ask about:
   - double rooms and cost for two nights
   - breakfast (included?)
   - location of hotel.

   Your name is: P. Machowski
   Credit card details:
   - Mastercard
   - 4352 8576 8346 1101
   - Expiry date: 04/15

File 52 | Unit 11

Business communication, Exercise 7, page 70

Student B

You are a visitor at the hotel. Check in and ask for information on the following.

- dinner in room?
- times for breakfast?
- swimming pool?
- Internet access in the hotel?

File 53 | Unit 12

Language at work, Exercise 8, page 75

Student B

Here is a list of your tasks for the week. Ask Student A if he / she has done his / her tasks and say if you have done yours.

Example: *B Have you ordered a new computer?*
A Yes, I have.

You	Done?	Student A
book venue for annual conference	no	order a new computer?
write minutes for team meeting	no	ship delivery to Argentina?
organize meeting with union rep	yes	telephone clients about new product?
ask boss for some time off	no	email new brochure to clients?

File 54 | Unit 12

Business communication, Exercise 4, page 76

Student B

You are in charge of information and design for the brochure.
You think it's going to take about six weeks to get all the information. The designers need about four weeks. You have annual leave between August 15th and 30th.

Discuss the final schedule and write down the stages with all the important dates.

File 55 | Unit 2

Starting point, page 12

Answers

1 Lufthansa – German; Sony – Japanese; Coca-Cola – American
2 Philips – electronics; Bayer – pharmaceuticals; Microsoft – software
3 Banco do Brasil – financial services; Allianz Worldwide Care – insurance; CNN – news

File 56 | Unit 3

Case study, Task, Exercise 1, page 23

Student C

	A	B	C
Location			centre of capital city, inside a shopping centre
Other businesses near			a lot of shops, banks, travel agents, fast food café
Transport			train, bus
Type of customers			shoppers
Parking			not good, expensive

File 57 | Unit 12

Business communication, Exercise 4, page 76

Student C

You are in charge of printing and postage.
The printers need about three weeks.
You think it's going to take about two weeks to send them out to customers.
You have annual leave between October 10th and 17th.

Discuss the final schedule and write down the stages with all the important dates.

File 58 | Unit 10

Business communication, Exercise 5, page 64

PAPOTECH	Possible solutions	Cost in €
Prices	Offer 10% lower prices on the 100 most popular products a) to all customers b) to our biggest customers	 100,000 45,000
Pay	Increase salaries a) by 10% b) by 5%	 50,000 25,000
Training	Give more training to call centre staff	10,000
Jobs	a) Recruit two new staff for the call centre b) Offer three staff the post of team leader	60,000 20,000
IT	a) Buy a new computer system b) Train staff to use the new system	100,000 15,000

File 59 | Unit 11

Business communication, Exercises 7 & 8, page 70

Metro Hotel Services

We are pleased to offer guests many services:

Room Service (310)
Order food in your room from 07.00–24.00

Wake-up call (311)
Telephone for an early morning wake-up call. We can also order taxis to the airport.

Breakfast (313)
Served in the restaurant from 07.00–09.30. (Also available in rooms)

Restaurant (313)
Book a table for dinner this evening at our French restaurant.

Business services (314)
One meeting room is available. Please book in advance.

Gym and sauna
On basement floor. Open 24 hours a day.

All rooms have
- wireless Internet access
- pay to view TV with eight film channels
- air conditioning.

Unit 1

01

Dahlia is Indian.
Raquel is Brazilian.
Randy is American.
Lukasz is Polish.
Tiziana is Italian.
Charlotte is British.
Yuko is Japanese.
Jacob is South African.

02

Japan
Japanese
British
Italy
Italian
India
American
Brazilian
Polish
Africa

03

1 I'm from India. I'm a receptionist for an American company.
2 Hello. I'm from Brazil. I'm a human resources manager. I work for an Italian company.
3 Hi. I'm a sales rep. I'm from the USA, but my company is Japanese.
4 Hello. I'm Polish and I'm a team leader for an Indian company.
5 Hi. I'm a personal assistant from Italy. I work for a Polish company.
6 Hello. I'm the Chief Executive Officer for a British company and I'm from the UK.
7 Hello. I'm Japanese. I'm a technician for a Brazilian company.
8 I'm a financial director from South Africa. I work for a South African company.

04

Interviewer So where is your company exactly?
Zuckerberg It's in Palo Alto, in California.
Interviewer You are a CEO, so are you at work all the time?
Zuckerberg Yes, I am. But my work colleagues are also my friends. For example, Dustin Moskovitz, Head of Engineering, is a friend from college. And Adam D'Angelo is my Chief Technology Officer. We're old friends from school.

06

1

A What's his name?
B Mr Gorski.
A How do you spell that?
B G-O-R-S-K-I.
A Thanks.

2

A What's your company?
B Lufthansa.
A How do you spell that?
B L-U-F-T-H-A-N-S-A.
A Thanks.

07

Alek Hello. My name is Alek Gorski. That's G-O-R-S-K-I. We have an appointment with Mrs Da Rocha.
Eva How do you do, Mr Gorski? I'm Eva, Maria Da Rocha's assistant.
Alek Pleased to meet you, Eva. This is my assistant, Elzbieta Wozniak.
Eva Nice to meet you, Elzbieta. Sorry – how do you spell that?
Elzbieta Elzbieta? That's E-L-Z-B-I-E-T-A.
Eva E-L-Z-B-I-E-T-A. Thanks. Just a moment. Maria, your visitors are here.

Maria Alek. It's good to see you again.
Alek And you. How are you?
Maria I'm fine. And you?
Alek Not so bad. Maria, do you know Elzbieta? She's my new assistant.
Maria No. How do you do, Elzbieta?
Elzbieta Pleased to meet you.

08

Maria See you soon, Alek.
Alek Yes, goodbye Maria.
Maria Nice meeting you, Elzbieta.
Elzbieta Nice meeting you, too.
Maria Bye. Have a good journey.
Alek Thanks. Bye.

Unit 2

09

William Nice to see you again, Natasha. Do you know Malik?
Natasha No. Hello, I'm Natasha Darcy. Nice to meet you.
Malik You too. Where do you work?
Natasha I'm with Perfect Match. It's a small recruitment company. We provide staff – especially in the pharmaceuticals industry. What about you?
Malik I work for a company called RiskLink. We produce software for financial services companies.
Natasha Oh right. What about you, William? Do you still work in electronics?
William Well, yes, but I don't have a job right now. That's why I'm here. I want to find something in the automobile industry, if possible.

10

pharmaceuticals
electronics
recruitment
hospitality
finance
automobile

11

Kikkoman is a Japanese company and we sell four hundred million litres of soy sauce every year. We employ six thousand, five hundred people in total. We export soy sauce all over the world, including Asia, North America, Australia, and Europe. We also develop new products for the pharmaceuticals industry. Restaurants, supermarkets, and Asian food shops buy our products and we also provide lessons in Japanese cooking – using Kikkoman products of course!

12

A

Our first business area is Food and Food Service. We produce sugar and cooking oil. The company has restaurants, cafés, and food shops. It provides meals for restaurants, schools, and hospitals.

B

A Our second business area is Bio Pharma. Here we produce pharmaceuticals and medicines.

B And do you export these products?

A Yes, we do. We export medicines to countries around the world. And we develop new biotechnological products.

C

A The third area, Entertainment and Media, is now the main business of CJ. The company produces films for the Korean market and abroad.

B Does the company import films too?

A Yes, it does. We import films from foreign production companies like DreamWorks, and we have eight cable TV channels in Korea and a chain of cinemas.

D

A The fourth business area is Home Shopping and Logistics. We provide a home shopping service for customers, twenty-four hours a day.

B Do customers buy on the Internet?

A Yes, they do, but also on satellite TV. We have a logistics centre. It provides transport and delivery services.

13

1

A Do you export these products?

B Yes, we do.

2

A Does the company import films too?

B Yes, it does.

3

A Does CJ provide financial services?

B No, it doesn't provide financial services.

4

A Do you import medicines?

B No, we don't. We export medicines.

14

1

A Can I have your phone number?

B Certainly. It's oh-seven-seven-eight, four-five-six, three-six-five.

2

A What's the price for that mobile phone?

B It's forty-five dollars sixty.

3

One thousand three hundred employees work here.

4

We started the company in two thousand and one.

15

A Hello, Giorgio's.

B Hello. Can I book a private room in your restaurant for next Monday, please? It's for a group of twenty.

A Twenty people? Yes, of course. Can you give me your name, please?

B Yes, sure. It's Toshiko Hori. But the booking is in the name of BKD …

B That's fine. So do you have set meals for groups?

A Yes, we do.

B Can you tell me the prices?

A Yes, certainly. Twenty-five pounds or thirty-five pounds.

B Can you repeat that, please?

A Twenty-five and thirty-five.

B OK. Um … it's for a group of twenty. Can I have a special price?

A I'm sorry, but we don't have special prices for food. But if you have wine, maybe we can do …

B Can you confirm my booking by email?

A Yes, of course. Can I have your email address, please?

B Sure. It's t dot hori at bkd …

A …sorry, can you speak more slowly?

B T dot hori at bkd dot …

A Sorry, can you spell Hori?

B It's H-O-R-I at bkd dot com.

16

A Hello, Giorgio's.

B Hello. Can I book a private room in your restaurant for next Monday, please? It's for a group of twenty.

A Twenty people? Yes, of course. Can you give me your name, please?

B Yes, sure. It's Toshiko Hori. But the booking is in the name of BKD …

B That's fine. So do you have set meals for groups?

A Yes, we do.

B Can you tell me the prices?

A Yes, certainly. Twenty-five pounds or thirty-five pounds.

B Can you repeat that, please?

A Twenty-five and thirty-five.

B OK. Um … it's for a group of twenty. Can I have a special price?

A I'm sorry, but we don't have special prices for food. But if you have wine, maybe we can do …

17

Euroffice Euroffice, Customer Service.

Customer Hello, I'd like some information, please.

Euroffice Yes, how can I help you?

Customer Do you have a catalogue to order from?

Euroffice No, we don't. But you can see all our products online.

Customer OK. Err, is the delivery free?

Euroffice For orders over thirty pounds, yes. Otherwise we charge three pounds ninety.

Customer Right, and do you do express delivery?

Euroffice We do next day delivery on orders over thirty pounds. Other orders take two days.

Customer And can we return products?

Euroffice Oh yes, you can return any product within fourteen days of delivery.

Customer OK, and finally do you do international deliveries?

Euroffice No, I'm afraid we only deliver in the UK.

Customer OK. That's all, thanks for the information.

Euroffice You're welcome. Goodbye.

Customer Bye.

Unit 3

18

Good morning. Today, I'd like to tell you about Spectrum Brands. We're a global company with our head office in Atlanta and a technical centre in Madison, Wisconsin. We do our research and development there. We also have twenty-one factories in North America and four more in Latin America: in Guatemala, Brazil, and Colombia. There are two factories in Europe: in Germany and the UK. Oh, and there's also one in China. Now moving on to sales, there are about forty sales offices worldwide. There are ten in North America, thirteen in Latin America, three in Asia-Pacific, fourteen in Europe, and one in Dubai for customers in the Middle East and Africa. We also have thirty-eight distribution and packaging centres around the world.

19

A Dubai is a great location for a conference. The weather is always good.
B What about the airport? Are there lots of international flights?
A Yes, there are. And there isn't a problem with transport from the airport because public transport is excellent in Dubai.
B But is there a good place for a conference?
A Yes, there is. It's the Dubai International Exhibition and Convention complex. It's perfect.

20

Receptionist Hello, the Dubai Grand Hotel. Can I help you?
Sadler Hello. This is Raymond Sadler of Sadler Business Services. I'm calling about your meeting rooms …

Receptionist ... and there's Internet access and a fax in each room.
Sadler That's great. Thanks for your help.
Receptionist You're welcome.
Sadler Goodbye.
Receptionist Goodbye.

21

1

A Can you spell that?
B Yes, it's Nzogoung. That's N-Z-O-G-O-U-N-G.
A So that's M-Z-O-G-U-N-G.
B No, it's N as in New York, Z, O, G, O as in Oslo, U, N, G.
A Oh, I'm sorry. N-Z-O-G-O-U-N-G.
B That's right.

2

A OK. Can I have a contact number?
B Yes, it's three nine nine, six three four four.
A So, that's three three nine, six three three four. Is that right?
B No, it's three double nine, six three double four.
A Sorry, three nine nine, six three four four.
B Yes.

22

A Hello.
B Hello. Could I speak to Teresa Baum, please?
A I'm sorry, but she isn't here this morning. Can I help you?
B Could I leave a message for her?
A Sure.
B It's Richard Andac.
A Can you spell that, please?
B A-N-D-A-C.
A So that's A-N-D-A-C.
B That's right. And I'm calling about our meeting. Can she call me back as soon as possible?
A OK. Can I have a contact number?
B Yes, it's double oh double four, two zero seven, three nine nine, six three four four.
A Sorry, that's double oh double four, two zero seven, three nine nine, six three four four. Is that right?
B Yes.
A OK. I'll give her your message, Mr Andac.
B That's great. Thanks for your help.
A You're welcome.
B Goodbye.

Unit 4

23

1

A Excuse me. I can't find the ticket office.
B You can use this ticket machine. Just insert your credit card here and touch the screen.
A Great. Thanks.

2

A Sorry, I need to switch off my mobile phone – the battery is low.
B It's OK. You can recharge it here.
A Oh. Thanks.

3

A Excuse me, I want to use the Internet, but I can't get a wireless connection.
B Can I see your laptop?
A Sure.
B OK. Click on the start menu and then on network … now you need to key in your password.
A I don't have a password!
B Oh. Well you can't log on to the Internet without a username and a password.

4

A I can't stop the photocopier!
B Press the red button.
A It doesn't work.
B Here, let me help ... oh no!

24

First of all, the warehouse computer receives customer orders. Then, the computer tells a robot to find the correct box. Next, the robot finds the box and delivers it to a human co-worker. After that, the person takes the correct items for the order. And finally, the robot returns the box and starts again.

25

Magda Sorry, can you help me?
Chen Sure.
Magda How do I use the new Intranet?
Chen Do you have a password?
Magda Yes, it's here. I'm trying to key it in, but it doesn't work.
Chen That's because the password is in lower case letters. Don't use upper case letters.
Magda Oh!
Chen That's it. So here is 'Company News'. And you can also send messages.
Magda How?
Chen First of all, click on 'My Intranet'. Next click on 'Messages'. So it's similar to email. You have an inbox and you can send messages to people at work. OK?
Magda That's great. Thanks.

Chen Do you want a hand?
Magda That would be good. I don't know how to log out now.
Chen Errr. Close your messages and then click on 'sign out'.

26

1

We rent audio and visual products to individuals and companies. We often have problems with people losing the products, so this technology helps us to know exactly where each item is.

2

You can buy a microphone that you put into it and it records audio, so I don't need to take notes in meetings. I also store a lot of my documents so I can access them from anywhere.

Unit 5

27

A Hi, Michelle. It's Rona.
B Oh, hello. How can I help?
A Well, Hanran Solutions telephoned. They received our invoice for an order of scanners, but they say it's wrong. Did you print a hard copy of the original order form?
B No, but I always save their order forms. Let me open the folder. Erm, what was the date on it?
A The third of May.
B That's strange. It isn't here. Sorry about that. One moment. Did they attach the document to an email?
A Yes. I think they sent the email on the third.
B OK, here's an email from Hanran Solutions on the third with an attachment.
A That sounds good.
B Yes, it's an order for twenty scanners.
A Great. Can you forward the email to me?
B Sure.

28

Janusz Sorry I'm late. I was at the presentation on branding.
Carlos Wasn't that last week?
Janusz No, it was this morning at the Century Hotel.
Carlos Oh. Was it interesting?
Janusz Yes, it was, and there were lots of good questions at the end. The breakfast was good too! Anyway, why weren't you in the office yesterday?
Carlos There were terrible problems with flights from Rome, so I ...

29

Piotr Hello?
Lydia Hi, Piotr. It's Lydia. You called.
Piotr Yes, I just wanted to check if you called Ron Peters.
Lydia Yes, I did. Yesterday.
Piotr What did he say? Is there a problem?
Lydia No, not really. He can do the presentation, but not in the morning.
Piotr Why didn't he want to speak then?
Lydia No idea. Anyway, I telephoned the Century Hotel. They have a free room at lunchtime.
Piotr That's fine. Did you book it?
Lydia No, I didn't. Sorry about that. I'll call them now and I'll check with Ron Peters.
Piotr Great. Thanks Lydia.

30

decide
decided
telephone
telephoned
want
wanted
call
called
invite
invited

31

1

A Hello, sorry I'm late. There were problems with my flight.
B That's OK.

2

A Did you call the Century Hotel?
B No, I didn't. Sorry about that. I was really busy last week.

3

A Did you email the report?
B No, I'm really sorry. I forgot.

32

Joe Joe speaking.
Mandy Hi, Joe. It's Mandy again.
Joe Hi, Mandy.
Mandy I'm sorry Joe, but we've got a problem with the order for Gosport. We did all the baseball bats and T-shirts yesterday, so I can ship them tomorrow. But the logos on the caps didn't work. The colours are wrong. We need to fix the machine today and print them again. I'm really sorry.
Joe OK. Don't worry. I know the Purchasing Manager at Gosport, so I'll speak to him and explain the situation. But can you help me? We need to give another delivery date for this.
Mandy Sure. I'll call the factory now and I'll let you know as soon as I can.
Joe That would be great. Thanks a lot.

Unit 6

33

Visitor This is nice.
Host Yes, I eat here about once a month. Do you like sushi? It's very good here.
Visitor Yes, I do, but ...
Waitress Hello, are you ready to order?
Host Yes, I think so. We'd like a bottle of sparkling water ... and would you like to order first?
Visitor OK. I'll have the grilled vegetables, please.
Waitress OK.
Host And I'd like some sushi, please.
Waitress OK, so grilled vegetables and sushi. Would you like salad or some French fries?
Visitor Not for me, thanks.
Host No, thanks.

Host How was your meal?
Visitor Very nice, thank you.
Host Would you like a dessert?
Visitor No, thanks. I'll have a coffee.
Host Me too ... excuse me?
Waitress Yes?
Host We'd like two coffees, please.
Waitress Sure.
Host And could I have the bill, please?

34

Enzo Hello, can I join you?
Giang Yes, please take a seat. My name's Giang Bai. How do you do?
Enzo My name's Enzo Matti.
Giang Is this your first time in Vietnam?
Enzo Yes, it is. I'm with a textile company in Italy. Here's my card.
Giang Thank you. Here's mine. So you're from Italy. That's a long way to travel. How long did your journey take?
Enzo Err, it took about forty-eight hours, I think. I came to Ho Chi Minh City last night, but I left Bologna two days ago. I flew to Milan and then to Shanghai. I had a day in Shanghai so I met some colleagues there yesterday.
Giang Were you on the ten o'clock flight last night?
Enzo That's right.
Giang Oh, we were on the same flight then!
Enzo Really?

35

Giang So how did you become a sales manager in textiles?
Enzo Well, my family was always in textiles. My father had his own company in Bologna and I worked for him.
Giang Why did you leave?
Enzo Well, I went to university and I studied Business Management. Then I wanted to work abroad, so I left the family company and spent time in the United States.
Giang So when did you join your current company?
Enzo In two thousand and three.

36

Simon Can I join you?
Nathalie Yes, of course.
Simon I hear you work for GST.
Nathalie Yes, that's right.
Simon My name's Simon Turing. I'm with Tulsa Filters. You're one of our customers.
Nathalie Ah yes. Pleased to meet you. I'm Nathalie Anderson, and this is my colleague, Brent.
Brent Nice to meet you.
Simon And you. So what do you think of the conference?
Nathalie The conference? Very interesting.
Simon Do you come here every year?
Nathalie No. This is my first time. But Brent here is a regular!
Simon Do you know a lot of people here, Brent?
Brent No, not many. The faces change every year. Erm, would you like another drink?
Simon No, thanks.
Nathalie No, thanks. I'm fine.
Brent Well, please excuse me. I need to go to my room before dinner.
Simon Sure. See you later maybe.

37

A Hello. Can I help you?
B Yes, please. I have an appointment with Mr Cannon, but there's nobody in Reception.
A Oh dear. Is this your first time here?
B Yes, it is.
A Well, come with me. I can take you to his office.
B Thanks very much. After you.

A OK, right … here's John Cannon's office. Please go in and take a seat.
B Thank you.
A I think John's just next door. I'll call him. Can I get you something? A coffee?
B Oh, yes, please.
A OK, I'll ask him to bring you one. Have a good meeting. Nice talking to you.
B Yes, and you. Bye.

Unit 7

38

works
is
manages
deals
plans
organizes
products
departments
computers
controls
develops
resources

39

Security Good morning sir.
Jim Hello, I have an appointment at Whitley's.
Security Do you want the factory or the offices?
Jim The offices.
Security Well, you go along this road and turn right. Go past the factory to the offices, but don't park there. Look for the car park sign and drive down below the offices and go into the car park there.
Jim That's great. Thanks a lot.

40

Jim Good morning. I have an appointment with Olivia Gonzalez.
Receptionist OK. What's your name, please?
Jim Jim Berman.
Receptionist One moment. Can you sign here, please?
Jim Sure.
Receptionist And this is your visitor's pass.
Jim OK. Thanks.
Receptionist Please take a seat. Ms Gonzalez will be right down.

Olivia Hello Jim.
Jim Hi Olivia. Nice to see you again.
Olivia Nice to see you, too. Did you find us OK?
Jim Yes, no problem. Your directions were very clear.
Olivia Good. Would you like a coffee first?
Jim Actually, I'm fine.
Olivia OK. Let me show you round.
Jim Great.

Olivia So, this is Production and that's the main production line.
Jim How many people work on it?
Olivia About thirty I think. But let me introduce you to Diego. He's in charge of Production ...

Unit 8

41

energetic
imaginative
careful
friendly
practical
focused
patient
experienced

42

Anton OK. So we have a student for the summer job. Let's discuss the web editor position next. Who do we have?
Sandra There were lots of emails for this one, but there are only two people really. First of all, there's Monica. I spoke to her on the phone and she's very friendly. At the moment she works in publishing.
Anton Is she an editor?
Sandra Yes. She has a lot of experience in book editing, but she says she's good at editing websites because she does some in her free time for friends and small businesses.
Anton OK. That sounds like a possibility. What about the other person?
Sandra Here's his picture. Do you recognize him?
Anton Yes, who is he?
Sandra It's Roberto. He was the student on our summer placement last year.
Anton That's right. Roberto! I remember him. Very energetic! Really nice young man.
Sandra Exactly. Anyway, now he has a qualification in IT.
Anton But why is he applying for the web editor job? He doesn't have any experience in editing and he isn't very good at working on his own.
Sandra I know, but he liked it here so much last summer he wants a job. I think he's perfect for the position of web production assistant.
Anton Exactly. Let's offer him that and then invite Monica for an interview. I'd like to see the websites she worked on as well.
Sandra Sure. I'll send you the links.

43

1

A Come on Sandra. It's twelve o'clock. Let's go for lunch.
B Sorry, I'm not going for lunch today. There's no time.
A Why? What are you doing?
B Anton and I are interviewing someone.
A What? Now?
B It's for the web editor position. She's waiting in Reception. Sorry. See you later.
A Bye.

2

A Where's Chantelle?
B She isn't working here today. She's at home.
A Why?
B She's finishing her report. Her boss wants it for seven thirty tomorrow morning.

3

A Where are Bill and Sofia going?
B They're doing the training course for that new finance software all day.
A When are they back?
B At about a quarter to six.

44

1

A Come on Sandra. It's twelve o'clock. Let's go for lunch.
B Sorry, I'm not going for lunch today. There's no time.
A Why? What are you doing?
B Anton and I are interviewing someone.
A What? Now?
B It's for the web editor position. She's waiting in Reception. Sorry. See you later.
A Bye.

45

2

A Where's Chantelle?
B She isn't working here today. She's at home.
A Why?
B She's finishing her report. Her boss wants it for seven thirty tomorrow morning.

3

A Where are Bill and Sofia going?
B They're doing the training course for that new finance software all day.
A When are they back?
B At about a quarter to six.

46

1

A Where are you going?
B Home.
A But it's only twelve o'clock.
B I know. But I'm working from home this afternoon.

2

A When are they back from the training course?
B At about five forty-five.

3

A She's working on that report today.
B When does her boss want it?
A For seven thirty tomorrow morning.

4

A What time does your train leave?
B At ten past eleven.

47

Kasia Hi Bruno. It's Kasia here.
Bruno Hi Kasia. How are you?
Kasia Fine, thanks. Listen, we need to meet about the plan for staff to work from home. Can we arrange a meeting on Thursday with Dolores and Chen? Is two o'clock OK for you?
Bruno Sorry, I'm busy then. What about the morning?
Kasia OK. What time are you free?
Bruno Nine thirty is good for me.
Kasia I can't meet between eight and ten. I've got interviews.
Bruno Are you busy after that?
Kasia Dolores and I have an appointment with someone from the bank at twelve, so let's meet before that.
Bruno Is ten fifteen good for you?
Kasia Yes, a quarter past ten on Thursday is fine, but I don't know about Dolores and Chen. I think Chen has a factory visit in the morning.
Bruno OK. Can you call Dolores and I'll phone Chen?
Kasia Sure.
Bruno Thanks. Bye.

Unit 9

48

Interviewer How big is the Accor group?

Manager Well, we employ one hundred and seventy thousand people in nearly a hundred countries. And we have over four thousand hotels worldwide.

Interviewer So, very big.

Manager Yes, we are, but the hotel industry is very competitive – there are a lot of big chains out there.

Interviewer That's true. So, with so many competitors, how does Accor stay competitive?

Manager Well, one reason is that we are the only international group with hotels in every market segment. This means we can offer all our customers a wide choice. For example, Motel Six is a chain of budget hotels in North America. They offer the customer a cheap option. Then at the economy level there's the All Seasons brand in the Asia-Pacific region. You pay more at these hotels, but they offer very good service with friendly staff.

Interviewer What about hotels for the business traveller who wants more comfort and services?

Manager OK. This is the mid-range market segment. So, we're talking about hotels like Novotel. The quality at a Novotel hotel is very high with modern, up-to-date business facilities like meeting rooms and office services. Location is also important for the customer at these hotels so they are easy to find in city centres or at international airports.

Interviewer And what if money is no problem for the customer?

Manager Then you choose a Sofitel hotel. It's expensive, but it offers five-star quality and each one also offers the visitor something else. Because each country is different, every Sofitel hotel is different and gives the customer a special experience.

49

1 We can offer all our customers a wide choice.
2 They are low-price hotels and offer the customer a cheap option.
3 They offer very good service with friendly staff.
4 The quality at a Novotel hotel is very high with modern, up-to-date business facilities.
5 A Sofitel hotel is expensive, but it offers five-star quality.

50

1

A Our competitive advantage is that we provide a better service.

B What do you mean exactly?

A Well, our staff are more experienced than our competitors' staff. They get six weeks' training before they start.

B So they can give good advice to your customers?

A Yes, that's right. And our staff are friendlier than other shops. We know our customers well because we often see them.

B What about the products?

A Well, when there's a new product on the market, we're always the first shop in town to stock it. Customers know that our products are more up-to-date. They come here first to see the technology.

2

B What are your competitive advantages?

C Well, the first one is the price. We offer lower prices than our competitors.

B That's because you don't have any shops?

C Yes, but also because we buy products in large quantities. We have thirty thousand cubic metres of storage space, so we have bigger stocks than all our competitors.

B Is that an advantage for delivery, too?

C Yes, of course. Because we have large stocks we provide faster delivery. We always deliver in two or three days. And we offer a wider choice – five thousand different products.

51

1

A We have a special low price on this model this month. Only twenty-nine euros ninety-nine.

B That's not bad.

A And then you pay only seventeen euros fifty a month. That's for ten hours of calls.

B Ten hours a month. I don't need ten hours.

A Well, if you prefer five hours a month, it's only eleven seventy-five.

2

A Is delivery free?

B Yes, it is, if you order more than five hundred dollars of goods.

A And if I don't?

B Then there's a delivery charge of seven dollars fifteen cents per item.

A So that's about thirty dollars for four items.

B Yes, twenty-eight sixty to be exact.

3

A That's two thousand, eight hundred and sixty yen, please.

B I have a customer card.

A OK, so that gives you a discount of one hundred and seventy yen today. So that's two thousand, six hundred and ninety yen.

52

Managing Director So, did you look at the two quotes for the website?

Javier Yes briefly. Err … here they are.

Managing Director OK. How do they compare?

Javier For price, ITE is cheaper.

Managing Director Yes, so I see. Why is that?

Javier They're a smaller, newer company. It's two brothers. Weblines is older and it has about twenty staff.

Managing Director Are they better?

Javier The quality is similar. Weblines produces very nice sites, but ITE also does good work. The advantage of ITE is the two people have experience in the online marketing and sales industry. The disadvantage of Weblines is they don't usually work with online businesses.

Managing Director How fast can they do the work?

Javier There's no difference. They both need four months.

Managing Director Four?

Javier That's fairly normal.

Managing Director I see. Well, what do you think?

Javier Erm. I prefer ITE. They're cheaper, they're professional, but also easy to talk to. I like their work – it's more modern.

Managing Director Fine. Let's choose them.

Javier Good. I'll call them today.

Unit 10

53

1

A Right. So, is that everything?

B Erm, there's a small problem with my assistant. She wants more money, but I can't give her a pay rise.

A Oh I see. Can she do some overtime?

B Yes. That's a good idea!

2

A What's the matter?

B I have a really big problem. The Managing Director wants to reduce staff numbers in my department. So someone has to lose their job. But who?

A That's a difficult decision.

B Yes, it is!

3

A So, what's your final decision?

B I don't know. I can't decide.

A Why don't you ask everyone in your team?

B No. That's a bad idea. There are eight people so we'd get eight different opinions. We'll never find a solution that way.

54

Richard Morning, Adriana. How was your weekend?

Adriana Fine, thanks.

Richard Is Jorge coming?

Adriana Yes, but he's speaking to the team leader on line two at the moment. I think he was late again.

Richard What? Again?

Adriana That's three times this month.

Richard OK, let's start. How are things on production line one?

Adriana Marcio, the team leader, says they are still having problems because the line is slow.

Richard Didn't the new components arrive on Friday?

Adriana No, but the supplier says they are arriving later today.

Richard And when are you going to the factory in Recife?

Adriana Tonight. I'm leaving at six.

Richard So, is Marcio dealing with the new components when you're in Recife?

Adriana Yes. He's fine. He can organize the changes.

Richard Good. Who are you meeting in Recife tomorrow?

Adriana Pedro, the Line Manager, and the team leaders.

Richard So what are the problems in Recife?

Adriana The biggest problem is that production's slow. Pedro says the new components don't work well.

Richard Are these the same components we're waiting for?

Adriana That's right!

55

Richard Hello.

Adriana Hi, Richard. It's Adriana.

Richard How are things in Recife?

Adriana Not good, I'm afraid. The problem is bigger than we thought.

Richard Oh no! Not because of the new components? They were so expensive!

Adriana No, I know they were the most expensive solution, but they were also the best idea.

Richard So what's the real problem?

Adriana Well, Pedro says the new components are worse than the old components, but the team leaders say they are better, and I agree.

Richard So are you saying the problem isn't technical?

Adriana That's right. I think it's a personnel problem. Do you know that staff turnover in Recife is the highest? Our other factories are about thirty per cent lower.

Richard Wow. That is surprising. So the problem is the team?

Adriana No, not the team. It's the Line Manager. The biggest problem is Pedro. No one likes him.

56

Oh no. That's terrible

Really? How amazing.

Great. That's fantastic!

Wow. That is surprising.

I'm sorry. How disappointing.

Good. That's excellent news.

57

Director So. Did you read the report?

Line manager Yes.

Director And? What's your opinion?

Line manager I think it explains some of the problems, but not all. For example, we have the highest prices, so in my opinion that's one reason. But some customers also say that our delivery times are slow.

Director I agree. And it isn't just delivery that's slow. Look at the figures for the call centre. We have the longest call times. Do you think they need more training?

Line manager I don't think so. All the staff get regular training. Maybe it's a problem of teamwork. I think we should make them feel part of a team where people like working.

Director Hmm. I'm not so sure.

Unit 11

58

A Hello. Is this the check-in for all BA flights?
B Yes, it is. Do you have your passport and ticket?
A Here you are.
B And how many bags are you checking in today?
A None. I just have hand luggage.
B OK. Would you like a window or an aisle seat?
A Err, aisle please.
B OK. So your flight leaves from gate forty-nine at six fifty-five, but boarding starts half an hour before. You're in seat five C.
A Thanks.

59

A When is your trip to Canada?
B Next week.
A Why are you going?
B To visit the sales offices. I'm going to visit Toronto first to see the sales reps there.
A Great. Are you going to Vancouver as well?
B No, I'm not going to have time. But I'm going to spend a day in Quebec to present the new product to Dominic and his team.
A Oh! Quebec is beautiful.
B Yes, I think we're going out in the evening to see the old city and have dinner.
A When are you coming back?
B On Thursday, but I'm going to take Friday off to have a nice long weekend.
A Good idea!

60

1

A Here you are. The terminal is there.
B Thanks. How much is that?
A Eighteen pounds, please.
B Er … here's twenty. Keep the change. Can I have a receipt?
A Sure.

2

A Can I help you?
B Err, I'd like something for my children. How much do these cost?
A They're twenty-nine euros each.
B OK. I need two. Can I pay by credit card?
A Sure.

3

A Hello. Can I help you?
B I'd like to change five hundred dollars into euros, please.
A Certainly. The exchange rate is one point two three today. Is that OK?
B Er … what's the total?
A Four hundred and six euros.
B OK.
A Do you want the notes in fifties?
B Yes, that's fine.
A So that's four hundred and six euros and your receipt.
B Thanks very much.

61

Receptionist Hello. Clarion Hotel.
Jenny Hello. I'm calling from Dublin airport. I've missed my flight, so I'd like to book a room for the night. Do you have any vacancies?
Receptionist Yes, we have a double room at one hundred and twenty euros.
Jenny Does that include breakfast?
Receptionist Yes, it does.
Jenny Great. Can I book a room, then?
Receptionist Certainly. Can I have your name?
Jenny It's Ms Chiang. C-H-I-A-N-G.
Receptionist And I need your credit card details.
Jenny Sure. It's Visa.
Receptionist And what's the card number?
Jenny 6674 8596 8374 6374.
Receptionist And the expiry date?
Jenny Zero three, fourteen.
Receptionist OK, Ms Chiang. That's a double room for just one night. You can check in any time now.
Jenny Sorry, where is the hotel exactly?
Receptionist We're on the airport grounds. There's a free bus from the terminal.
Jenny Thanks very much. See you later.

62

1

Receptionist Good evening, madam.
Jenny Hello. My name is Chiang. I have a reservation for tonight.
Receptionist That's right. Can I see your credit card, please?
Jenny Here you are.
Receptionist Thank you. Your room is on the fifth floor. Room five-oh-one. The lift is over there.
Jenny Thanks. What time is breakfast served?
Receptionist It's between five and ten a.m. There's also dinner in the hotel restaurant this evening until ten.
Jenny Do I need to book a table?
Receptionist No, you don't.

2

Receptionist Hello. Reception.
Jenny Hello. This is Ms Chiang in room five-oh-one. Can I have a wake-up call, please?
Receptionist Certainly. What time is that for?
Jenny Six a.m., please. Also, can you order me a taxi to the airport terminal for seven o'clock?
Receptionist Yes, we can arrange that.
Jenny Sorry, there's one other thing. Do the rooms have Internet access? I can't log on.
Receptionist Yes, they do, but there's a problem with the connection this evening. Sorry, we're trying to fix it now.
Jenny OK. I'd also like dinner in my room. Do you have room service?
Receptionist Yes, one moment, please ...

Unit 12

63

Greta Hello, Greta Helsing speaking.

Barati Hi Greta, it's Barati in Kathmandu.

Greta Oh, hi Barati.

Barati Hi. Thanks for your email about the Palmarosa oil. We've sent it and it's going to arrive on the twenty-seventh. I know you have a tight deadline, but we've had a few problems here.

Greta Don't worry. The twenty-seventh is OK. I can change the schedule by a week.

Barati Have you taken lots of orders for the soap?

Greta Yes, there's been a lot of interest.

Barati Great. Have you seen some of the other products on our website?

Greta Yes, I have. They look really interesting.

Barati You should come and visit us sometime. Have you ever been to Nepal?

Greta No, I haven't, but I'd love to!

64

Greta At the moment, the schedule is about a week late. The situation is that the raw material from Nepal has just arrived and we've already taken it to the warehouse. So the aim is to get the soap on the shelves by Valentine's Day.

Soledad But what's the deadline for this? I know we need it for February the fourteenth, but what date is the launch?

Greta We plan to launch it on January the twentieth.

Soledad But Martin, how much time do we need for production?

Martin Production isn't a problem. But we haven't got a final package yet.

Greta I know. I've spoken to the designers again today. We'll have the packaging by the thirty-first of October.

Martin OK. So we'll have the final product by the end of December?

Greta That's right. Around the twentieth.

Soledad Why don't we deliver the product at the beginning of January? The shops are going to want it earlier than the twentieth.

Greta OK. Then, let's start delivery from the warehouse on January the second. Is everyone happy with that date?

Martin / Soledad Fine. No problem.

Greta Right. So, to summarize, I'm going to call our packaging people – again. And we're going to tell clients they'll have the product by January the ...?

Soledad Let's say January the fifth. I'll tell them. And I'm going to prepare some press releases as well.

Greta Great.

OXFORD
UNIVERSITY PRESS

Great Clarendon Street, Oxford OX2 6DP

Oxford University Press is a department of the University of Oxford. It furthers the University's objective of excellence in research, scholarship, and education by publishing worldwide in

Oxford New York

Auckland Cape Town Dar es Salaam Hong Kong Karachi Kuala Lumpur Madrid Melbourne Mexico City Nairobi New Delhi Shanghai Taipei Toronto

With offices in

Argentina Austria Brazil Chile Czech Republic France Greece Guatemala Hungary Italy Japan Poland Portugal Singapore South Korea Switzerland Thailand Turkey Ukraine Vietnam

OXFORD and OXFORD ENGLISH are registered trade marks of Oxford University Press in the UK and in certain other countries

First published 2009
2016 2015
20 19 18 17 16 15 14

ISBN: 978 0 19 474801 8 (Book)
ISBN: 978 0 19 473937 5 (Pack)

Printed in China

This book is printed on paper from certified and well-managed sources.

ACKNOWLEDGEMENTS

The authors and publisher are grateful to those who have given permission to reproduce the following extract and adaptation of copyright material: p 72 quotation from an interview with Prescott Bowden. Reproduced by kind permission of Prescott Bowden.

Sources: http://english.cj.net/; www.kikkoman.com; www.spectrumbrands.com; www.virgintrains.co.uk; www.fujitsu.com; www.tankseveryday.com; www.unilever.com; www.designbuild-network.com; www.accor.com; www.morrisons.co.uk; www.iht.com; www.cityrunningtours.com; www.strandtravel.co.uk

Fictitious interview with Mark Zuckerberg based on factual information from: www.fastcompany.com/magazine/

Illustrations by: Mark Duffin pp 24, 25, 31; Becky Halls/The Organisation pp 45, 51, 69; Martin Sanders/Mapart.co.uk pp 6, 44, 45, 91, 106, 114.

We would also like to thank the following for permission to reproduce the following photographs: Alamy pp 12 (electronics/rtpartner-images.com), 12 (real estate/ Pictures Colour Library), 12 (automobile/Friedrich Stark), 12 (hospitality/View Stock), 12 (financial services/Amazing Images), 13 (container ship /Arco Images GmbH), 14 (cinema box office/Kelly Jett), 17 (pencils and paperclips /Garry Gay), 19 (factory/vario images GmbH & Co.KG), 29 (iPhone/Alex Segre), 29 (computer game/David L. Moore – Lifestyle), 29 (Blue-tooth earpiece/Image Source Black), 29 (iPod/Joe Bird), 30 (pen tablet/Jupiterimages/Comstock Images), 32 (Simon Rawles), 34 (Bernhard Classen), 36 (outdoor cafe/Ian Dagnall), 37 (sandwich/ Photo Agency Eye), 40 (cocktail party/PhotoAlto Agency RF Collections/ Frederic Cirou), 49 (aerobics/Jupiterimages/Polka Dot), 49 (lifeboat/PBPA Paul Beard Photo Agency), 49 (nursery/Janine Wiedel Photolibrary), 51 (working at computer/Frank Chmura), 60 (climber/Eric von Michael), 60 (rafting/Buzz Pictures), 66 (queue inside plane/Oote Boe Photography 2), 74 (Iconotec), 106 (airport/Crispin Rodwell), 106 (presentation/Big Cheese Photo LLC), 114 (hotel room/Dirk v. Mallinckrodt), 114 (sandwiches/WoodyStock), 114 (meeting/Yuri Arcurs/INSADCO Photography); Ardea.com p 42 (bees/Steve Hopkin); Axiom p 53 (masks/Paul Quayle); Corbis pp 18 (golf course and cactus/ Tony Roberts), 38 (Simon Marcus), 47 (spiral stairway/John Harper), 66 (security check/Reuters), 106 (hotel suite/Bob Krist), 106 (historic city/Jon Hicks); Frank Lane Picture Agency p 30 (dolphins/Flip Nicklin/Minden Pictures); Courtesy of Fujitsu Europe Ltd p 30 (snap scanner); Getty Images pp 6 (mosaic/Jed Share), 6 (Dahlia/Zubin Shroff), 6 (Yuko/Keith Brofsky/UpperCut Images), 11 (dancers/ Peter Essick), 12 (container port/Lester Lefkowitz), 12 (software/Tom Grill), 13 (lab technician/David Joel), 19 (conveyor belt/John Lund/Drew Kelly), 19 (laboratory/Hans Neleman), 19 (office workers/ERproductions Ltd), 20 (Johnny Greig), 22 (Loungepark), 23 (city street/Jerry Driendl), 29 (circuit board/Jody Dole), 29 (sat nav/Creative Studio Heinemann/Westend61), 35 (Chinese jugglers/Richard Nowitz), 36 (Chinese restaurant/Hans Neleman), 37 (sushi/Gregor Schuster), 40 (woman waiting /Yellow Dog Productions), 43 (air traffic controller/Lester Lefkowitz), 43 (teacher/Shannon Fagan), 43 (engineer /Lester Lefkowitz), 43 (team leader /Hans Neleman), 43 (production manager /Colorblind), 48 (construction workers/Nicolas Russell), 49 (doctor/ Mustafa Ozer/AFP), 54 (skaters/Doug Pensinger), 54 (hotel/AFP/Stringer), 59 (vegetables/ColorBlind), 60 (violinists/AFP), 62 (Richard/Hans Neleman), 62 (Pedro/Mark Edward Atkinson), 66 (plane and clouds/Lester Lefkowitz), 68 (Neil Massey), 71 (mosaics/Courtney Milne), 72 (tulips/Takashi Sato), 103 (businesswoman/Patti McConville), 103 (businessman/Jun Takahashi), 103 (business couple/Thomas Barwick), 110 (businesswoman/Patti McConville), 110 (businessman/Jun Takahashi), 110 (business couple/Thomas Barwick), 114 (airport/Peter Adams); Jupiterimages pp 14 (meal tray/Timespace), 37 (salad/Brian MacDonald Photography), 37 (cheese/Jupiter Images), 37 (chips/ Spathis Miller), 37 (steak/Scott Peterson); Courtesy of Kiva Systems p 26 (Staples warehouse at Denver); Photolibrary.com pp 13 (soy sauce/Joy Skipper), 13 (preparing sushi/Tim Imrie), 19 (office builder/Dennis Gilbert), 41 (canapes/ Jan Baldwin), 49 (architect/Strauss/Curtis Strauss/Curtis); Punchstock pp 6 (Raquel/Image Source), 6 (Randy/Westend61), 6 (Lukasz/Image Source), 6 (Tiziana/Michael Blann/Digital Vision), 6 (Charlotte/Noel Hendrickson/Digital Vision), 6 (Jacob/Andersen Ross/Blend Images), 9 (Esta and Orial/Nick Clements/ Digital Vision), 10 (PhotoAlto/Laurence Mouton), 12 (pharmaceuticals/Jupiter/ Brand X), 12 (Recruitment/Comstock Imagaes), 14 (online shopping/Rolf Bruderer/Blend Images), 18 (Stockbyte), 18 (Don Farrall/Photodisc), 28 (Tetra Images), 29 (portable dvd/Dan Dalton/Digital Vision), 37 (cup of coffee/Ross Anania/Photographer's Choice), 37 (coffee beans /Purestock), 62 (Adriana/ ColorBlind/Digital Vision), 65 (woman pushing chair/Dave & Les Jacobs/Blend Images), 77 (ripples/Stuart McCall/Photographers Choice), 106 (buffet/Vegar Abelsnes Photography/Digital Vision), 114 (city/Justin Lightley/Photographer's Choice); Reuters pp 8 (Kimberly White), 24 (CERN hadron collider/Denis Balibouse), 56 (Yuriko Nakao); Rex Features p 24 (Virgin train/Rex); Science Photo Library p 14 (medicine/Volker Steger); Courtesy of Spectrum Brands p 18 (Rayovac, Remington and Varta)

Images sourced by: SuzanneWilliams/Pictureresearch.co.uk

Cover photo: Chris King

The authors and publisher would also like to thank the following individuals for their advice and assistance in developing the material for this book: Linda fenton, Nina Leeke, Giovanna Kim, Flemming Winther Nielsen, Jo Kirihara, Liam Higgins, Penny McLarty, Renu Pholsward, Robert Anderson, Stewart Chalmers.